366 WAYS TO PEACE

Quotations & Scripture
Compiled by Melodie M. Davis

Herald
Press

Scottdale, Pennsylvania
Waterloo, Ontario

12-4. In *Whole People, Whole Earth*, 1:21.

12-5. In Bartlett, 13th ed., 926.

12-6. *Making Peace in the Global Village*, 15.

12-7. *Faith in a Nuclear Age*, 126.

12-8. *Complete Writings of Menno Simons*, 555.

12-9. "Learning to Raise a Peacemaker," *Sojourners*, 4/1992, 38.

12-10. *The Way God Fights*, 74.

12-11. *Way to Inner Peace*, 83.

12-12. *Roots; in Seeds of Peace*, 162.

12-13. In *Seeds of Peace*, 261.

12-14. CFMP, "Commentary," 82.

12-15. *Way to Inner Peace*, 179.

12-16. In *Seeds of Peace*, 206.

12-17. In *Seeds of Peace*, 233.

12-18. In *Peace: On Not Leaving It to the Pacifists*, 74.

12-19. In *Readings from Mennonite Writings*, 77.

12-20. "Learning to Raise a Peacemaker," *Sojourners*, 4/1992, 41.

12-21. In *Seeds of Peace*, 263.

12-22. In *Seeds of Peace*, 114.

12-23. "Prince of Peace for All," in *Readings from Mennonite Writings*, 107.

12-24. "Prayer for Peace," *Thomas Merton on Peace*, 267.

12-25. *Thomas Merton on Peace*, 111, referring to Isa. 9:6; Eph. 2:14.

12-26. "To Us a Child of Hope Is Born," *Mennonite Hymnal*, # 125.

12-27. CFMP, 81.

12-28. CFMP, 82.

12-29. In *Images of Peace*, 16.

12-30. *But Why Don't We Go to War?* (Herald Press, 1992), 200.

12-31. In *Seeds of Peace*, 270.

The Compiler

Melodie M. Davis is the author of eight books and the syndicated columnist of "Another Way." She grew up in a Mennonite family, learning ways of peace from her parents, and graduated from Eastern Mennonite University. Since then, she has served as a writer at Harrisonburg, Virginia, for Mennonite Media, a department of Mennonite Board of Missions. Melodie and her husband, Stuart, are the parents of three daughters and belong to Trinity Presbyterian Church, Harrisonburg.

366 WAYS TO PEACE
Perpetual calendar
Copyright © 1999 by Herald Press, Scottdale, PA 15683
Published simultaneously in Canada by Herald Press, Waterloo, Ont. N2L 6H7
Credits given on pages after Dec. 31
All rights reserved
ISBN: 0-8361-9113-7
Printed in the USA
Art and design by Gwen M. Stamm
07 06 05 04 03 02 01 00 99 10 9 8 7 6 5 4 3 2 1

To order or request information, please call 1-800-759-4447 (individuals);
1-800-245-7894 (trade). Website: www.mph.org

11-2. *N. T. Basis of Peacemaking*, 23.
11-3. In *Ten Fighters for Peace*, 91.
11-4. *You Are My Hiding Place*, 25-26.
11-5. *The Idea of Disarmament*, 187.
11-6. *The Different Drum*, 188.
11-7. In *Readings from Mennonite Writings*, 1992.
11-8. *Making Peace in the Global Village*, 15.
11-9. Angelo Giuseppe Roncalli, pope 1958-63.
11-10. *Way to Inner Peace*, 51.
11-11. *Peace: On Not Leaving It to the Pacifists*, 4.
11-12. *Peace Keeping or Peace Making?* 11.
11-13. In *Readings from Mennonite Writings*, 327.
11-14. In *Seeds of Peace*, 161.
11-15. *Cry Pain, Cry Hope*, 39.
11-16. In *Whole People, Whole Earth*, 1:20.
11-17. In Bartlett, 13th ed., 372.
11-18. Unpublished audiotape, 1993.
11-19. *Way to Inner Peace*, 147.
11-20. In *Seeds of Peace*, 247.
11-21. *The Way of Peace*, 68.
11-22. In *Seeds of Peace*, 209.
11-23. "I Bind My Heart This Tide," *Mennonite Hymnal*, # 353.
11-24. *The Prophet* (1923); in Bartlett, 13th ed., 924.
11-25. *The Way God Fights*, 71.
11-26. In *Seeds of Peace*, 215.
11-27. *Aphorisms on Man* (ca. 1788); in Bartlett, 13th ed., 372.
11-28. In *Seeds of Peace*, 62.
11-29. *Making Peace in the Global Village*, 15.
11-30. *Complete Writings of Menno Simons*, 558.
12-1. *Way to Inner Peace*, 143.
12-2. *Cry Pain, Cry Hope*, 33.
12-3. *You Are My Hiding Place*, 90.

Preface

You are about to walk for a year in the company of thinkers who, for the most part, have lived out their commitment to peacemaking. They have made profound and powerful statements for peace.

People in all walks of life and with many points of view can benefit from this calendar. Its quotations have been selected from a Christian and Anabaptist-Mennonite perspective. They are for both seasoned peacemakers—inspiration for the long haul—and for beginners in learning what it means to be peacemakers.

Rather than tamper with now-famous quotes, I have chosen to keep original wording intact, as in using "men" to refer to everyone. Many of these notables, if alive today, would be at the forefront of using inclusive language.

Not everyone will agree with the choice of people quoted. Yet we have no right to judge the lives of those we have not known. Even scoundrels say and do some things we applaud. Overall, I have included speakers whose actions and words have in some way moved us toward a world at peace.

—*Melodie M. Davis*

10-1. In *Whole People, Whole Earth*, 1:20.

10-2. *Meditations for Lent*, 148.

10-3. In *Whole People, Whole Earth*, 2:47.

10-4. In James H. Forest, "Merton's Peacemaking," *Sojourners*, 12/1978; in *Images of Peace*, 8.

10-5. *Your Child's Self-Esteem* (New York: Dolphin Books, Doubleday, 1975); in *Images of Peace*, 10.

10-6. *Faith in a Nuclear Age*, 126.

10-7. In *The Anabaptists Are Back*, foreword.

10-8. *Anabaptism: Neither Catholic nor Protestant* (Waterloo, Ont.: Conrad Press, 1973), 83.

10-9. From a speech.

10-10. In *Earth Prayers from Around the World*, 367.

10-11. MCC, Akron, Pa.

10-12. "Let There Be Light, Lord God of Hosts," *Church Hymnal*, # 304.

10-13. In *N. T. Basis of Peacemaking*, 72.

10-14. Compiler's daughter.

10-15. In *Peace: On Not Leaving It to the Pacifists*, 73.

10-16. In *Seeds of Peace*, 175.

10-17. In *Readings from Mennonite Writings*, 231.

10-18. *Departure*, 36.

10-19. CFMP, 85-86.

10-20. *Peace: On Not Leaving It to the Pacifists*, 84.

10-21. *Prayer Is a Hunger* (Denville, N.J.: Dimension Books, 1972); in *Images of Peace*, 20.

10-22. In *Images of Peace*, 50.

10-23. *Christopher News Notes*, 1-2/1982, no. 259; in *Images of Peace*, 46.

10-24. Karol Wojtyla, pope 1978-; in *Images of Peace*, 54.

10-25. *Seeds of Contemplation*, 73.

10-26. In *Ten Fighters for Peace*, 142.

10-27. In *Peace: On Not Leaving It to the Pacifists*, 66.

10-28. *N. T. Basis of Peacemaking*, 20.

10-29. *Peace, War, and the Christian Conscience*; in *Images of Peace*, 22.

10-30. Indira Gandhi.

10-31. *The Confessions of a Daddy* (1907), chap. 1; in Bartlett, 13th ed., 843.

11-1. "Let There Be Light, Lord God of Hosts," *Church Hymnal*, # 304.

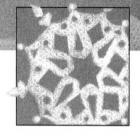

JANUARY 1
New Year's Day

World Day of Prayer for Peace

If you want to make peace, you must
be peaceful.
—*Peace Pilgrim*

Dear children, let us not love with words or tongue
but with actions and in truth.
—*1 John 3:18, NIV*

8-31. *The Words of Gandhi*, 55.

9-1. *The Wisdom of M. L. King, Jr.*, 102; in *Stride Toward Freedom*, 102.

9-2. In *Readings from Mennonite Writings*, 131.

9-3. "Peace, Perfect Peace," *Church Hymnal*, # 455.

9-4. *Peace Keeping or Peace Making?* 26.

9-5. CFMP, 82.

9-6. In *Seeds of Peace*, 223.

9-7. In *Seeds of Peace*, 174.

9-8. *Complete Writings of Menno Simons*, 507.

9-9. "God the Omnipotent," *Mennonite Hymnal*, # 86.

9-10. In *Seeds of Peace*, 219.

9-11. *Complete Writings of Menno Simons*, 94, adapted.

9-12. In *Seeds of Peace*, 177.

9-13. *Selections from the Journal of George Fox*, Great Devotional Classics (Nashville: The Upper Room, 1951), 17.

9-14. In *The Anabaptists Are Back*, 114.

9-15. In *Readings from Mennonite Writings*, 343.

9-16. "Evening."

9-17. In *All God's People* video, MBM Media Ministries, 1990.

9-18. In *Seeds of Peace*, 214.

9-19. "O Day of God, Draw Nigh," *Mennonite Hymnal*, # 88.

9-20. *Wisdom of M. L. King, Jr.*, 175; "True Peace," Atlanta, July 5, 1962.

9-21. *The Words of Gandhi*, 20.

9-22. "Let There Be Light, Lord God of Hosts," *Church Hymnal*, # 304.

9-23. *An Account of the Manners of the German Inhabitants of Pennsylvania* (Philadelphia, 1875), 62.

9-24. In the *New Yorker*; in *Preaching on Peace*, 17.

9-25. *Preaching on Peace*, 5, preface.

9-26. *Dare to Reconcile*, 20.

9-27. In *Seeds of Peace*, 177.

9-28. In *Seeds of Peace*, 210.

9-29. *Faith in a Nuclear Age*, 76.

9-30. "In Christ There Is No East or West," *Mennonite Hymnal*, # 387.

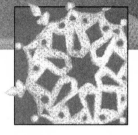

JANUARY 2

True communication, like the charity it requires, begins at home. Perhaps peace-making should start small.
—*M. Scott Peck*

If I speak in the tongues of mortals and of angels, but do not have love, I am a noisy gong or a clanging cymbal.
—*1 Corinthians 13:1, NRSV*

7-31. In *Ten Fighters for Peace*, preface.

8-1. In *Seeds of Peace*, 158.

8-2. Unpublished audiotape, 1993.

8-3. In Bartlett, 15th ed., 780.

8-4. "Unity," *Sing and Rejoice*, # 129.

8-5. In *Champion of World Peace* (N.Y.: Julian Messner, 1962).

8-6. In *Ten Fighters for Peace*, 38.

8-7. *Faith in a Nuclear Age*, dedication.

8-8. In *Seeds of Peace*, 248.

8-9. "A Change of Heart: Billy Graham on the Nuclear Arms Race," *Sojourners*, 8/1979, 14.

8-10. In *Salt and Pepper*, 100.

8-11. "O Young and Fearless Prophet," *Mennonite Hymnal*, # 459.

8-12. In *Ten Fighters for Peace*, 85.

8-13. In *Seeds of Peace*, 146.

8-14. In *The Sacred Pipe*. See Acknowledgments, above.

8-15. In *Seeds of Peace*, 160.

8-16. *Peace Pilgrim*, 16.

8-17. In *Peace Heroes*, 256.

8-18. *Complete Writings of Menno Simons*, 198.

8-19. In *Ten Fighters for Peace*.

8-20. *Way to Inner Peace*, 93.

8-21. *Faith for a Secular World*, 23.

8-22. "Prayer Alone Will Sustain Peacemakers over the Long Run," *Catholic Bulletin*, Jan. 13, 1981; in *Images of Peace*, 24.

8-23. In *Seeds of Peace*, 162; cf. Exod. 21:23-24; Lev. 24:19-20; Matt. 5:38-42.

8-24. *Thomas Merton on Peace*, 111.

8-25. *Faith in a Nuclear Age*, 69.

8-26. "God of Grace and God of Glory," *Mennonite Hymnal*, # 434.

8-27. Heading over two cartoons in Washington *Times Herald* after World War I; in *Ten Fighters for Peace*, 68.

8-28. Unpublished audiotape, 1993.

8-29. *Lest Innocent Blood Be Shed* (New York: Harper & Row, 1979), 287.

8-30. *Peace Keeping or Peace Making?* 22.

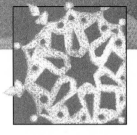

JANUARY 3

Forgiveness is not an occasional act; it is
a permanent attitude.
—*Martin Luther King Jr.*

Forgive us our sins, for we also forgive everyone
who sins against us.
—*Luke 11:4a, NIV*

6-30. *Seeds of Contemplation*, 72.

7-1. In *Ten Fighters for Peace*, 36.

7-2. *The Different Drum*, 19.

7-3. *Peace Pilgrim*, 17.

7-4. In *Peace Heroes*, 208.

7-5. In *Seeds of Peace*.

7-6. *The Ways of Peace*, 11.

7-7. *Way to Inner Peace*, 95.

7-8. *Devotions upon Emergent Occasions* (1624), # 17; in Bartlett, 15th ed., 254.

7-9. *Waiting for God* (New York: Harper & Row, 1973), 115.

7-10. "The Rime of the Ancient Mariner," *The Poems of Samuel Taylor Coleridge*, Oxford Standard Authors Series (London: Oxford Univ. Press, 1912), 299.

7-11. In *Seeds of Peace*, 152.

7-12. In *Seeds of Peace*, 153.

7-13. *Peace Thinking in a Warring World*, 25.

7-14. *Peacemakers: Christian Voices*, 5.

7-15. *The Words of Gandhi*, 18.

7-16. In *Seeds of Peace*, 144.

7-17. *The Different Drum*, 329.

7-18. *Peace Pilgrim*, 162.

7-19. In *Peace Heroes*, 249.

7-20. In *Readings from Mennonite Writings*, 262.

7-21. In *Seeds of Peace*, 124.

7-22. In *Seeds of Peace*, 145.

7-23. *Meditations for Lent*, 147.

7-24. "A Peace Community in Ireland," "Your Time" leaflet, MBM, 1981.

7-25. *Images of Peace*, preface.

7-26. *Traits of a Healthy Family* (Minneapolis: Winston Press, 1983); in *Images of Peace*, 52.

7-27. *Dwell in Peace*, 25. See Acknowledgments, above.

7-28. *Seeds of Contemplation*, 182.

7-29. In *Christopher World* (N.Y.: The Christophers); in *Images of Peace*, 58.

7-30. Compiler's father.

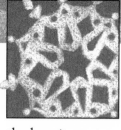

JANUARY 4

Once people understand the strength of nonviolence—the force it generates, the love it creates, the response it brings from the total community—they will not easily abandon it.

—*Cesar Chavez, organizer of underpaid farm workers*

No one takes my life from me, but I lay it down of my own accord. I have authority to lay it down and authority to take it up again.

—*John 10:18, NIV, adapted*

5-30. In *Christian Living,* Jan. 1994, 17.

5-31. *The Words of Gandhi,* 57.

6-1. In *Seeds of Peace,* 245.

6-2. *Way to Inner Peace,* 94.

6-3. *Caring Enough to Forgive* (Herald Press, 1981), 52.

6-4. CFMP, "Commentary," 83.

6-5. *The Different Drum,* 326.

6-6. In *Peace Heroes,* 208.

6-7. In *Seeds of Peace.*

6-8. *The Words of Gandhi,* 101.

6-9. *The Wisdom of M. L. King, Jr.,* 81; in *The Strength to Love,* 112.

6-10. *Vultures and Butterflies* (Herald Press, 1992).

6-11. In *Seeds of Peace,* 160.

6-12. In *Seeds of Peace,* 235.

6-13. In *Peacemakers: Christian Voices,* 23.

6-14. *The Anabaptists Are Back,* ed. Duane Ruth-Heffelbower (Herald Press, 1991), 114.

6-15. *You Are My Hiding Place,* 90.

6-16. *The Complete Writings of Menno Simons,* trans. Leonard Verduin, ed. J. C. Wenger (Herald Press, 1956, 1984), 554.

6-17. *Nonresistance and Responsibility,* 64-65.

6-18. In *Readings from Mennonite Writings,* 343.

6-19. In R. H. Bainton, *Here I Stand* (Nashville: Abingdon, 1950), 185.

6-20. Confucius.

6-21. *Way to Inner Peace,* 93.

6-22. *The Wisdom of M. L. King, Jr.,* 173; in *Stride Toward Freedom,* 98.

6-23. In Sophie Jewett, *God's Troubadour* (New York: Thomas Y. Crowell Company, 1938), © Edith Jewett.

6-24. *Seeds of Contemplation,* 104.

6-25. In *Peacemakers: Christian Voices,* 23.

6-26. *Peace Thinking in a Warring World,* 96.

6-27. *Dare to Reconcile,* 52, adapted.

6-28. "A Christian Conscience About War," 4.

6-29. Quoting Mark 12:30.

JANUARY 5

Peace is a chorus singing in harmony.
—*Jamie Hovey, ninth-grader*

Children are a gift from God.
—*Psalm 127:3a, TLB*

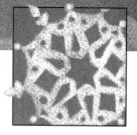

4-29. Article, *McCall's,* Oct. 1966; in Bartlett, 15th ed. (1980), 761, n. 3.
4-30. In *Peace Heroes,* 193.
5-1. In Dorothy Nathan's *Women of Courage;* in *Seeds of Peace,* 112.
5-2. CFMP, "Commentary," 82.
5-3. *The Different Drum,* 326.
5-4. *Thomas Merton on Peace,* 104.
5-5. In *Seeds of Peace,* 107.
5-6. In *Images of Peace,* 80.
5-7. In *The Idea of Disarmament,* 197.
5-8. In *Peace: On Not Leaving It to the Pacifists,* 13.
5-9. *Rumor of Angels;* in *Peace: On Not Leaving It to the Pacifists,* 6.
5-10. In *Seeds of Peace,* 269.
5-11. "A Christian Conscience About War," 3.
5-12. *Making Peace in the Global Village,* 111.
5-13. *Faith for a Secular World,* 29.
5-14. In *Seeds of Peace,* 168.
5-15. In Elizabeth Roberts, *Earth Prayers from Around the World* (San Francisco: Harper S. F., 1991), 184.
5-16. John Adams.
5-17. In *Seeds of Peace,* 7.
5-18. Nov. 1969; in *Ten Fighters for Peace,* 109.
5-19. *Way to Inner Peace,* 93.
5-20. "Outwitted"; in Bartlett, 15th ed., 671.
5-21. In *Seeds of Peace,* 246.
5-22. *Departure* (Herald Press, 1991), 23.
5-23. Anonymous.
5-24. *Faith in a Nuclear Age,* 69.
5-25. *Peace Pilgrim,* 167.
5-26. *The Way God Fights* (Herald Press, 1987), 73.
5-27. "The Vision of Sir Launfal," *The Poems of Lowell,* Cambridge ed. (Boston: Houghton Mifflin Co., 1925), 111; cf. Matt. 25:40.
5-28. *Way to Inner Peace,* 51.
5-29. *Les Miserables,* 1862; in Bartlett, 13th ed., 497.

JANUARY 6
Epiphany

We believe that . . . God's peace is most fully revealed in Jesus Christ, who is our peace and the peace of the whole world. Led by the Holy Spirit, we follow Christ in the way of peace, doing justice, bringing reconciliation, and practicing nonresistance even in the face of violence and warfare.
—*Confession of Faith in a Mennonite Perspective*

For no one can lay any foundation other than the one that has been laid; that foundation is Jesus Christ.
—*1 Corinthians 3:11, NRSV*

3-29. In *Seeds of Peace*, 148.

3-30. In *Seeds of Peace*, 132.

3-31. *Peace Thinking in a Warring World*, 99.

4.1. In *Seeds of Peace*, 268.

4-2. *Faith in a Nuclear Age*, 126.

4-3. *Teach Us How to Pray* (New York: Paulist, 1967); in *Images of Peace*, 74.

4-4. In *Seeds of Peace*, 263.

4-5. *The Cloud of Unknowing* (14th cent.), trans. Wm. Johnston (New York: Image Books, Doubleday, 1996).

4-6. "Let There Be Peace on Earth," *Sing and Rejoice!* compl. and ed. Orlando Schmidt (Herald Press, 1979), # 53.

4-7. Giovanni Battista Montini, pope 1963-78, in *Preaching on Peace*, 11.

4-8. In *Whole People, Whole Earth*, 2:47.

4-9. *The Words of Gandhi*, 57.

4-10. In *Seeds of Peace*, 26.

4-11. In *Seeds of Peace*, 167.

4-12. In *Seeds of Peace*, 244.

4-13. "Words from 1993," *Mennonite Weekly Review*, Dec. 30, 1993, 4.

4-14. *Peace Thinking in a Warring World*, 111.

4-15. E. C. McKenzie, compiler, *Salt and Pepper* (Grand Rapids: Baker Book House, 1977), 100.

4-16. *Peacemakers: Christian Voices*, 5.

4-17. *The Writings of P. M.*, ed. Wm. Klassen et al. (Herald Press, 1978).

4-18. In *Images of Peace*, 38.

4-19. In *Why I Am a Mennonite*, ed. H. Loewen (Herald Press, 1988), 250.

4-20. In *Salt and Pepper*, 100.

4-21. *Peace Keeping or Peace Making?* 57.

4-22. In *Seeds of Peace*, 118.

4-23. *Way to Inner Peace*, 147.

4-24. *Images of Peace*, preface.

4-25. In *Peacemakers: Christian Voices*, 22.

4-26. "Pacifism Is a Gift of God," 3.

4-27. *Thomas Merton on Peace*, 161-162.

4-28. GC Mennonite Church, Newton, Kan.

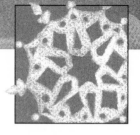

JANUARY 7

Love thine enemy but confront his evil.
—*Joan Baez*

Bless those who persecute you;
  bless and do not curse them.
—*Romans 12:14, NRSV*

2-28. *Self Reliance;* in John Bartlett, ed., *Familiar Quotations,* 13th ed. (Boston: Little, Brown and Co., 1955), 501.

2-29. "Learning to Raise a Peacemaker," *Sojourners,* 4/1992, 41.

3-1. *The Words of Gandhi,* 89.

3-2. "A Christian Conscience About War," 17.

3-3. In *Seeds of Peace,* 266.

3-4. *Peace Keeping or Peace Making?* 19.

3-5. *Preaching on Peace,* 5, in the preface.

3-6. *The Gospel of Peace,* 188.

3-7. In *Peace, On Not Leaving It to the Pacifists,* 74.

3-8. In *Peace Heroes in Twentieth-Century America,* ed. Charles DeBenedetti (Bloomington: Indiana Univ. Press, 1986), 165.

3-9. *The Words of Gandhi,* 76.

3-10. "When Peace Like a River," *Church Hymnal,* # 452.

3-11. "Pacifism Is a Gift of God," *Gospel Herald,* Feb. 1, 1994, 2.

3-12. In *Seeds of Peace,* 170.

3-13. In *Seeds of Peace,* 36.

3-14. In *Seeds of Peace,* 248.

3-15. In *Ten Fighters for Peace,* 20.

3-16. *Seeds of Contemplation,* 47.

3-17. *Dwell in Peace,* 13. See Acknowledgments, above.

3-18. "Peace Pentecost," *Sojourners,* 3/1982; in *Images of Peace,* 50.

3-19. "Words from 1993," *Mennonite Weekly Review,* Dec. 30, 1993, 4.

3-20. In *Seeds of Peace,* 173.

3-21. In *Seeds of Peace,* 216.

3-22. *N. T. Basis of Peacemaking,* 120.

3-23. *Way to Inner Peace,* 25.

3-24. *Peace, On Not Leaving It to the Pacifists,* 3.

3-25. *The New Testament Basis of Pacifism* (N.Y.: Fellowship of Reconciliation, 1936), 40.

3-26. Friend of compiler.

3-27. In *Ten Fighters for Peace,* 89.

3-28. In Joan Baez's autobiography *Daybreak;* in *Ten Fighters for Peace,* 127.

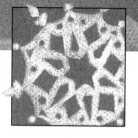

JANUARY 8

Help us to be masters of the weapons
that threaten to master us.
—*Thomas Merton*

No weapon forged against you will prevail, and you will refute
every tongue that accuses you. This is the heritage of the
servants of the Lord, and this is their vindication from me,"
declares the Lord.
—*Isaiah 54:17, NIV*

1-28. In *Seeds of Peace*, 111.
1-29. *Making Peace in the Global Village*, 15.
1-30. Graymoor Ecumenical and Interreligious Institute, Garrison, N.Y.
1-31. In *Seeds of Peace*, 209.
2-1. "Handbook for World Peacemaker Groups." In Long Jr., *Peace Thinking in a Warring World*, 96.
2-2. *The Different Drum*, 328.
2-3. "Prayer for Peace," in *Thomas Merton on Peace*, 268.
2-4. In *Seeds of Peace*, 104.
2-5. *Peace: On Not Leaving It to the Pacifists*, 83.
2-6. "In the Rifted Rock," *Church Hymnal*, # 454.
2-7. In *Peace Times*, Apr. 1992, Center for Teaching Peace. PCCS, Castle Rock, Minn.
2-8. *Cry Pain, Cry Hope*, 39.
2-9. In *Seeds of Peace*, 169.
2-10. In *Seeds of Peace*, 269.
2-11. *Where Do We Go from Here?* 182.
2-12. In *Seeds of Peace*, 161.
2-13. *Faith in a Nuclear Age* (Herald Press, 1983), 17.
2-14. *The Town Beyond the Wall*.
2-15. In *Ten Fighters for Peace*, 87.
2-16. *Peace, War, and the Christian Conscience* (N.Y.: The Christophers, 1982); in Pat C. Hinton, *Images of Peace* (Minneapolis: Winston Pr., 1984), 23.
2-17. "On Loving the Russians," *Sojourners*, 11/1982; in *Images of Peace*, 16.
2-18. *Peace Keeping or Peace Making?* 18.
2-19. Papal letter, "Peace on Earth," in *N. T. Basis of Peacemaking*, 140.
2-20. "Pax Romana and Pax Christi," in *Preaching on Peace*, 95.
2-21. *The Ways of Peace*, 12.
2-22. *Faith for a Secular World*, 17.
2-23. In *Please Save My World? In Seeds of Peace*, 76.
2-24. *Praying* (Minneapolis: Winston Press, 1979); in *Images of Peace*, 4.
2-25. *Way to Inner Peace*, 58.
2-26. In *Peacemakers: Christian Voices*, 22.
2-27. Unpublished audiotape, 1993.

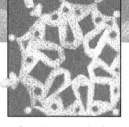

JANUARY 9

The witness of young conscientious objectors has been an inspiration to many of us. In a very honest and human fashion, they simply took the teachings of Jesus at face value and sought to live according to them. . . . They simply said that they would not kill, that war is wrong.
—*Sigurd Lokken*

No one should wrong or exploit a brother or sister in this matter, because the Lord is an avenger in all these things.
—*1 Thessalonians 4:6, NRSV, adapted*

Credits by the Day

1-1. *Peace Pilgrim* (Santa Fe: Ocean Tree, 1983), 5.

1-2. *The Different Drum* (N.Y.: Touchstone, Simon & Schuster, 1987), 17.

1-3. *The Wisdom of Martin Luther King, Jr.*, ed. Alex Ayres (Burtonville, Md.: Meridian Books), 83.

1-4. In *Seeds of Peace*, 169. See Acknowledgments, above.

1-5. In *Seeds of Peace*, 262.

1-6. *CFMP*, 81.

1-7. In *Ten Fighters for Peace: An Anthology*, ed. Don Lawson (New York: Lothrop, Lee & Shepard Co., 1971), 141.

1-8. "Prayer for Peace," in *Thomas Merton on Peace*, 268. See Acknowledgments, above.

1-9. In *Peace: On Not Leaving It to the Pacifists*, 20.

1-10. In *Peacemakers: Christian Voices from the New Abolitionist Movement*, ed. Jim Wallis (San Francisco: Harper & Row, 1983), 23.

1-11. Bumper sticker.

1-12. *Making Peace in the Global Village*, 74.

1-13. "Heart with Loving Heart United," *Mennonite Hymnal*, # 386.

1-14. In *Whole People, Whole Earth*, 1:47.

1-15. *The Wisdom of M. L. King, Jr.*, 174.

1-16. In *Seeds of Peace*, 210.

1-17. *New Testament Basis of Peacemaking* (Herald Press, 1979), 140.

1-18. In *Seeds of Peace*, 174; cf. Luke 23:34.

1-19. In *Seeds of Peace*, 74.

1-20. *Peace Keeping or Peace Making?* 57.

1-21. *Way to Inner Peace* (New York: Doubleday, 1955), 1.

1-22. In *Seeds of Peace*, 113.

1-23. *The Words of Gandhi*, 44.

1-24. In *Please Save My World! Children Speak Out Against Nuclear War*, ed. Bill Adler (New York: Arbor House, 1984); in *Seeds of Peace*.

1-25. In *Seeds of Peace*, 214.

1-26. In *Ten Fighters for Peace*, 17.

1-27. In J. C. Wenger, *The Way of Peace*, 16.

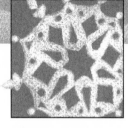

JANUARY 10

There have been times in the past when I have, I suppose, confused the kingdom of God with the American way of life. . . . I am grateful for the heritage of our country. . . . But the kingdom of God is not the same as America, and our nation is subject to the judgment of God just as much as any other nation.

—*Billy Graham*

Declare the Lord's glory among the nations
  his marvelous works among all the peoples.
—*Psalm 96:3, NRSV, adapted*

Merton, Thomas. *Seeds of Contemplation*. New York: © The Abbey of Gethsemani, Inc., 1949. Reprinted by permission of New Directions Publishing Corp.

_____. *Thomas Merton on Peace*. New York: © New Directions Publishing Corp., 1971.

Nelson, John Oliver. *Dare to Reconcile: Seven Settings for Creating Community*. New York: © Friendship Press, Inc., 1969.

O'Connor, Elizabeth A. *Cry Pain, Cry Hope*. 1650 Columbia Rd., NW, Washington, D.C.: © Servant Leadership School, 1993 rev.

Pedersen, Gerald O., ed. *Peace: On Not Leaving It to the Pacifists*. Philadelphia: Fortress, 1975, © Augsburg Fortress.

Rutenber, Culbert G. *Peace Keeping or Peace Making?* New York: © Friendship Press, Inc., 1968.

Sider, Ron J., and Darrel J. Brubaker. *Preaching on Peace*. Philadelphia: Fortress, 1982, © Augsburg Fortress.

Whole People, Whole Earth. Shalom Lifestyles Video Curriculum, 2 vols. Harrisonburg, Va.: © Mennonite Board of Missions Media Ministries, 1991.

Wiesel, Elie, ©. *The Town Beyond the Wall*. Boston Univ. Reissue: New York: Schocken Books, 1955, trans. Stephen Becker.

Wenger, J. C. *The Way of Peace*. Harrisonburg, Va.: © Mennonite Board of Missions (MBM) Media Ministries, 1977.

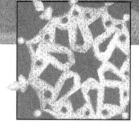

JANUARY 11

Visualize world peace.
—*Bumper sticker*

Of the increase of his government and peace there will be no end. The Prince of Peace will reign on David's throne and over his kingdom, establishing and upholding it with justice and righteousness from that time on and forever. The zeal of the Lord Almighty will accomplish this.
—*Isaiah 9:7, NIV, adapted*

Cox, Gray, © 1986. *The Ways of Peace: A Philosophy of Peace as Action*. Mahwah, N.J.: Paulist Press.

Derstine, Gerald. "Unity." In *Sing and Rejoice*. Scottdale, Pa.: © Herald Press, 1979.

Haas, J. Craig, compiler. *Readings from Mennonite Writings New and Old*. Intercourse, Pa.: © Good Books, 1992.

Gandhi, Mahandas. *The Words of Gandhi*. Selected by Richard Attenborough. New York: © Newmarket Press, design and selection, 1982; and Bombay: Navajivan Trust.

Geyer, Alan, © 1982. *The Idea of Disarmament*. Elgin, Ill.: The Brethren Press.

Kaufman, Gordon D. *Nonresistance and Responsibility, and Other Mennonite Essays*. Newton, Kan.: © Faith & Life Press, 1979.

Kirk, James G., © 1988. *Meditations for Lent*. Louisville: Westminster John Knox.

Larson, Jeanne, and Madge Micheels-Cyrus. *Seeds of Peace*. Philadelphia: © New Society Publishers, 1986 (1-800-333-9093).

Long, Edward LeRoy Jr., © 1983. *Peace Thinking in a Warring World*. Philadelphia: Westminster (John Knox).

Mauser, Ulrich. *The Gospel of Peace*. Louisville: © Westminster John Knox, 1992.

Mennonites. *Church Hymnal*. Scottdale, Pa.: © Mennonite Publishing House, 1927.

_____. *Confession of Faith in a Mennonite Perspective (CFMP)*. Scottdale, Pa.: © Herald Press, 1995.

_____. *The Mennonite Hymnal*. Scottdale, Pa.: © Mennonite Publishing House, 1969.

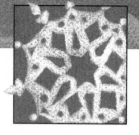

JANUARY 12

To the poor, violence is an empty stomach.
—*Robert McAfee Brown*

If a brother or sister is naked and lacks daily food, and one of you says to them, "Go in peace; keep warm and eat your fill," and yet you do not supply their bodily needs, what is the good of that?
—*James 2:15-16, NRSV*

Acknowledgments and Credits

Scripture is used by permission, with all rights reserved, from—

NIV: *The Holy Bible, New International Version* ®, copyright © 1973, 1978, 1984 by International Bible Society, Zondervan Publishing House.

NRSV: *New Revised Standard Version Bible*, copyright © 1989 by the Division of Christian Ed. of the National Council of the Churches of Christ in the USA.

TLB: *The Living Bible*, © 1971, owned by assignment by Illinois Regional Bank N.A. (as trustee), Tyndale House Publishers, Inc., Wheaton, IL 60189.

Quotations from Mennonites, Anabaptists, and other peace advocates are gratefully acknowledged by the compiler, Melodie M. Davis, and by Herald Press. They are used by permission of the authors or publishers, all rights reserved. Many of them have generously donated such use as a contribution for peace:

Arnett, Ronald C. *Dwell in Peace.* Elgin, IL 60120: © (copyright) The Brethren Press, 1980.

Augsburger, Myron S. *Faith for a Secular World.* Waco, Tex.: © Word Books, 1968.

Brown, Joseph Epes. *The Sacred Pipe: Black Elk's Account of the Seven Rites of the Oglala Sioux. Adapted.* Norman: © Univ. of Oklahoma Press, 1953.

Brown, Robert McAfee. *Making Peace in the Global Village.* Philadelphia: Westminster, 1981, © Westminster John Knox.

Carmichael, Amy. *You Are My Hiding Place.* Arranged by David Hazard. Minneapolis: © Bethany House Publishers, 1991.

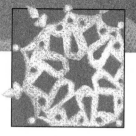

JANUARY 13

Kindle in us love's compassion,
  so that everyone may see,
In our fellowship the promise
  of the new humanity.
—*Nikolaus Ludwig von Zinzendorf*

Contribute to the needs of the saints; extend hospitality
to strangers.
—*Romans 12:13, NRSV*

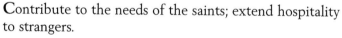

DECEMBER 31

Someday, after we have mastered the
winds, the waves, the tides and gravity, we
shall harness for God the energies of love.
Then for the second time in the history of the world,
man will have discovered fire.
—*Pierre Teilhard de Chardin*

Nation will not take up sword against nation,
    nor will they train for war anymore.
—*Isaiah 2:4, NIV*

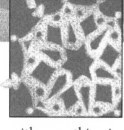

JANUARY 14

I think that Christ called us to that kind of difficult position of not identifying with everything in our society. He called us to stand out.
—*David Moser*

Do not love the world or the things in the world. The love of the Father is not in those who love the world.
—*1 John 2:15, NRSV*

DECEMBER 30

We are all on a journey, taking steps along the path of peace. It really doesn't matter where we are on that path, only that we are preparing for the next step. The danger is staying in the same place too long.
—*Susan Mark Landis*

Teach me your way, O Lord,
   and I will walk in your truth;
give me an undivided heart,
   that I may fear your name.
—*Psalm 86:11, NIV*

Martin Luther King's Birthday

One day we must come to see that peace
is not merely a distant goal we seek, but that it is a means
by which we arrive at that goal. We must pursue peaceful
ends through peaceful means.

—*Martin Luther King Jr.*

Happy are those who find wisdom,
    and those who get understanding. . . .
Her ways are ways of pleasantness,
    and all her paths are peace.

—*Proverbs 3:13, 17, NRSV*

What a privilege to have been brought to
this point, to be the generation that saves
God's creation and does what Jesus told us to
do two thousand years ago.
—*Dr. Helen Caldicott*

O God, the nations have come into your inheritance; . . .
Help us, O God of our salvation. . . .
Deliver us, and forgive our sins, for your name's sake. . . .
Then we your people, the flock of your pasture,
    will give thanks to you forever;
from generation to generation we will recount your praise.
—*Psalm 79:1, 9, 13, NRSV*

JANUARY 16

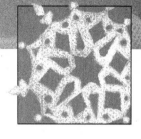

No one has a right to sit down and feel hopeless. There's too much work to do.
—*Dorothy Day*

So . . . live for the rest of your earthly life no longer by human desires but by the will of God.
—*1 Peter 4:2, NRSV*

DECEMBER 28

We give our ultimate loyalty to the God of grace and peace, who guides the church daily in overcoming evil with good, who empowers us to do justice, and who sustains us in the glorious hope of the peaceable reign of God.

—*Confession of Faith in a Mennonite Perspective*

If a kingdom is divided against itself, that kingdom cannot stand. And if a house is divided against itself, that house will not be able to stand.

—*Mark 3:24-25 NRSV*

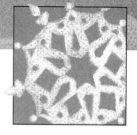

JANUARY 17

With God's help, we do not need to
choose death or killing. We can depend
on God to help us if we trust in God—
not in weapons of death.
—*Richard McSorley*

I will listen to what God the Lord will say;
he promises peace to his people, his saints—
    but let them not return to folly.
—*Psalm 85:8, NIV*

DECEMBER 27

A joyous song of peace announced Jesus' birth. Jesus taught love of enemies, forgave wrongdoers, and called for right relationships. . . . By his death and resurrection, he has removed the dominion of death and given us peace with God. Thus he has reconciled us to God and has entrusted to us the ministry of reconciliation.
—*Confession of Faith in a Mennonite Perspective*

Where, O death, is your victory?
Where, O death, is your sting?"
The sting of death is sin,
    and the power of sin is the law.
—*1 Corinthians 15:55-56, NIV*

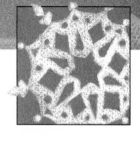

JANUARY 18

It can't be measured on the Richter scale,
but can you fathom the power of [Jesus']
words from the cross?
  "Forgive them; they know not what they do."
—*Lynn S. Larson*

When the centurion and those with him . . . saw the earthquake
and all that had happened, they were terrified, and exclaimed,
"Surely he was the Son of God!"
—*Matthew 27:54, NIV*

DECEMBER 26

His name shall be the Prince of Peace,
  For evermore adored.
—*John Morison*

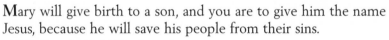

Mary will give birth to a son, and you are to give him the name Jesus, because he will save his people from their sins.
—*Matthew 1:21, NIV, adapted*

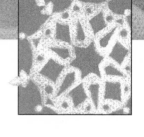

JANUARY 19

Being a pacifist between wars is as easy as being a vegetarian between meals.
—*Ammon Hennacy*

God is faithful, and he will not let you be tested beyond your strength, but with the testing he will also provide the way out so that you may be able to endure it.
—*1 Corinthians 10:13, NRSV*

DECEMBER 25
Christmas Day

We know that Christ came into this world as the Prince of Peace. Christ himself is our peace.
—*Thomas Merton*

A child has been born for us,
    a son given to us;
authority rests upon his shoulders;
    and he is named
Wonderful Counselor, Mighty God,
    Everlasting Father, Prince of Peace.
—*Isaiah 9:6, NRSV*

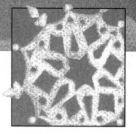

Nothing done for Christ is ever really
a failure, for all such efforts are gathered
up and remembered gratefully in God's
good heart.
—*Culbert G. Rutenber*

Therefore confess your sins to one other, and pray for one
another, so that you may be healed. The prayer of the righteous
is powerful and effective.
—*James 5:16, NRSV*

DECEMBER 24

In your will is our peace.
—*Thomas Merton, praying to God*

Let the peace of Christ rule in your hearts,
since as members of one body you were called to peace.
And be thankful.
—*Colossians 3:15, NIV*

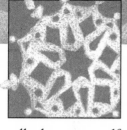

JANUARY 21

Here is a psychological suggestion for acquiring peace of soul. Never brag; never talk about yourself; never rush to first seats at table or in a theater; never use people for your own advantage; never lord it over others as if you were better than they.

—*Fulton John Sheen*

For by the grace given me I say to every one of you: Do not think of yourself more highly than you ought, but rather think of yourself with sober judgment, in accordance with the measure of faith God has given you.

—*Romans 12:3, NIV*

DECEMBER 23

Real peace can come to this world only in [Jesus'] name and in following him.
—*Hendrick B. Kossen*

Do not let your hearts be troubled:
Believe in God,
believe also in me.
—*Jesus, in John 14:1, NRSV*

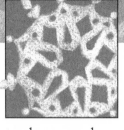

JANUARY 22

We have a long, long way to go. So let us hasten along the road, the roads of human tenderness and generosity. Groping, we may find one another's hands in the dark.

—*Emily Greene Balch*

I will come to you and fulfill my gracious promise to bring you back to this place. For I know the plans I have for you," declares the Lord, "plans to prosper you and not to harm you, plans to give you hope and a future."

—*Jeremiah 29:10-11, NIV*

DECEMBER 22

People who develop the habit of thinking
of themselves as world citizens are fulfilling
the first requirement of sanity in our time.
—*Norman Cousins*

Great is the Lord and most worthy of praise;
  he is to be feared above all gods.
For all the gods of the nations are idols,
  but the Lord made the heavens.
—*Psalm 96:4-5, NIV*

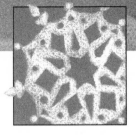

JANUARY 23

Nonviolence should never be used as a shield for cowardice. It is a weapon for the brave.
—*Mohandas K. Gandhi*

Be strong and take heart,
  all you who hope in the Lord.
—*Psalm 31:24, NIV*

DECEMBER 21

I still believe that people are really good at heart. . . . I see the world gradually being turned into a wilderness, I hear the ever-approaching thunder; . . . and yet, if I look up into the heavens, I think it will all come out right, that this cruelty too will end, and that peace and tranquillity will return again.
—*Anne Frank*

I will make a covenant of peace with them; it shall be an everlasting covenant with them; and I will bless them and multiply them, and will set my sanctuary among them forevermore.
—*Ezekiel 37:26, NRSV*

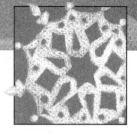

Peace is love that is passed on from
generation to generation.
—*Clifford, age 8*

Lord, you have been our dwelling place
throughout all generations.
—*Psalm 90:1, NIV*

DECEMBER 20

Parents who preach peace between warring
siblings may realize that their own behavior
is inconsistent with the peace that they try
to impose.
—*Cynthia J. Carney*

Peace be to you,
  and peace be to your house,
  and peace be to all that you have.
—*1 Samuel 25:6, NRSV*

JANUARY 25

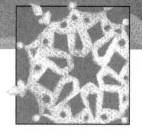

Every public reform was once a private opinion.
—*Ralph Waldo Emerson*

The Lord preserves the faithful,
   but abundantly repays the one who acts haughtily.
—*Psalm 31:23b, NRSV*

DECEMBER 19

This little spark [love], however small it may be in a person, does not come from humankind but from the source of Perfect Love.
—*Hans Denck*

No one has ever seen God; but if we love one another, God lives in us and his love is made complete in us.
—*1 John 4:12, NIV*

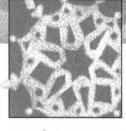

JANUARY 26

From the teachings of Buddha, Christ, Gandhi, from the dictates of their own consciences, many of today's young people have gradually come to believe that war is so singularly stupid and meaningless—not only in an immediate sense but also in the long view of history—that no thinking person should have anything to do with it.
—*Don Lawson, member of the U.S. Air Force during World War II*

Do not conform any longer to the pattern of this world, but be transformed by the renewing of your mind. Then you will be able to test and approve what God's will is—his good, pleasing and perfect will.
—*Romans 12:2, NIV*

DECEMBER 18

An affirmation of faith: . . . peace is
possible. This is our commitment, the faith
we seek to share.
—*Charles P. Lutz*

They will not hurt or destroy
    on all my holy mountain;
for the earth will be full of the knowledge of the Lord
    as the waters cover the sea.
—*Isaiah 11:9, NRSV*

JANUARY 27

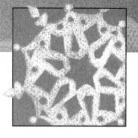

I cannot serve as a soldier. I cannot do evil.
I am a Christian.

—*Maximilian, executed at age 21 for not putting
on the uniform of the Roman army, A.D. 295*

Peter and the apostles answered, "We must obey God rather
than any human authority."

—*Acts 5:29, NRSV*

DECEMBER 17

We must do what we can. All of us can do something.
—*Oscar Romero*

In all your ways acknowledge the Lord,
    and he will make your paths straight.
—*Proverbs 3:6, NIV, adapted*

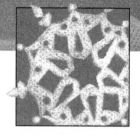

JANUARY 28

We have learned that we cannot live alone, at peace; that our own well-being is dependent upon the well-being of other nations, far away.
—*Franklin Delano Roosevelt*

Draw near, O nations, to hear;
    O peoples, give heed!
Let the earth hear, and all that fills it;
    the world, and all that comes from it.
—*Isaiah 34:1, NRSV*

DECEMBER 16

All we need for the triumph of evil is that good people do nothing.
—*Edmund Burke*

Depart from evil, and do good;
  seek peace, and pursue it.
—*Psalm 34:14, NRSV*

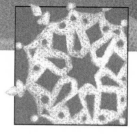

JANUARY 29

Whatever is unjust threatens peace.
Whatever fosters justice is an act of
peacemaking.
—*Robert McAfee Brown*

This is what the Lord says:
  "Maintain justice and do what is right,
  for my salvation is close at hand."
—*Isaiah 56:1, NIV*

DECEMBER 15

The condition for a happy life is to so live
that the trials . . . of life do not impose
their moods on us.
—*Fulton John Sheen*

Happy are the people to whom such blessings fall;
   happy are the people whose God is the Lord.
—*Psalm 144:15, NRSV*

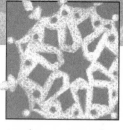

JANUARY 30

O God, . . . we pray for your church in the world. . . . Empower its witness, heal its divisions, make visible its unity. Lead us . . . so that, united in one body by the one Spirit, we may together witness to the perfect unity of your love.

—*Prayer of the Fifth World Conference on Faith and Order*

May they be brought to complete unity to let the world know that you sent me and have loved them even as you have loved me.

—*John 17:23, NIV*

DECEMBER 14

Peace embraces all of life. It includes personal peace with God, peace in human relations, peace among races and nations, and peace with the whole of God's creation.
—*"Commentary" on Confession of Faith*
  in a Mennonite Perspective

Keep on loving each other as brothers and sisters.
—*Hebrews 13:1, NIV, adapted*

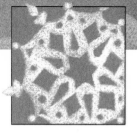

JANUARY 31

I will act as if what I do makes a
difference.
—*William James*

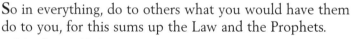

So in everything, do to others what you would have them
do to you, for this sums up the Law and the Prophets.
—*Matthew 7:12, NIV*

DECEMBER 13

It is crucial that we begin to understand
peace to mean, not only an end to war, but
an end to all the ways we do violence to
ourselves, each other, the animals, the earth.
—*Pam McAllister*

O Lord, who may abide in your tent?
    Who may dwell on your holy hill?
Those who walk blamelessly, and do what is right,
    and speak the truth from their heart.
—*Psalm 15:1-2, NRSV*

FEBRUARY 1

I commit myself to search for an ever-deepening understanding and appropriation of Christ's gift of inner security and peace.
—*Gordon Cosby and Bill Price*

I am the vine, you are the branches. Those who abide in me and I in them bear much fruit, because apart from me you can do nothing.
—*John 15:5, NRSV*

DECEMBER 12

When you clench your fist, no one can put anything in your hand, nor can your hand pick up anything.
—*Alex Haley*

In your anger do not sin": Do not let the sun go down while you are still angry.
—*Ephesians 4:26, NIV*

Focus your energy and being on what you
are for (peace, love, community) rather
than what you are against (military
industrialists, child abusers, organized crime).
—*M. Scott Peck*

In the same way, let your light shine before others, so that
they may see your good works and give glory to your Father
in heaven.
—*Matthew 5:16, NRSV*

DECEMBER 11

The greatest spiritual profit comes from loving those who hate us, and from giving gifts and dinners to those who cannot give anything in return, for then recompense will be made in the kingdom of heaven.
—*Fulton John Sheen*

Love your enemies, do good, and lend, expecting nothing in return. Your reward will be great, and you will be children of the Most High; for he is kind to the ungrateful and the wicked.
—*Luke 6:35, NRSV*

FEBRUARY 3

Help us to use our science for peace and plenty, not for war and destruction. Show us how to use atomic power to bless our children's children, not to blight them.
—*Thomas Merton*

As the new heavens and the new earth that I make will endure before me," declares the Lord, "so will your name and descendants endure."
—*Isaiah 66:22, NIV*

DECEMBER 10

We can envision a community of God
never preparing for war again, but using
what were once the weapons of war
to produce food for humankind.
—*Lois Barrett*

Come, let us go up to the mountain of the Lord,
　to the house of the God of Jacob;
that he may teach us his ways
　and that we may walk in his paths.
—*Isaiah 2:3, NRSV*

FEBRUARY 4

Nuclear weapons: may they rust in peace.
—*Bumper sticker*

In accordance with the Lord's promise, we wait for new
heavens and a new earth, where righteousness is at home.
—*2 Peter 3:13, NRSV, adapted*

DECEMBER 9

Children have much to teach us about
peacemaking and God's presence. Their
seemingly unlimited contact with creation
and the Creator is blessedly free of liturgical rules,
politically correct guidelines, or papal encyclicals.
—*Cynthia J. Carney*

The Lord will guide you always;
he will satisfy your needs in a sun-scorched land
  and will strengthen your frame.
—*Isaiah 58:11a, NIV*

FEBRUARY 5

Christians speak not just of a "way to peace," but of that peace which is "the way," the way to a fulfilled life together in the world "God so loved." Peace is not an absence but a presence.

—*Gerald O. Pedersen*

Through Christ we have gained access by faith into this grace in which we now stand. And we rejoice in the hope of the glory of God.

—*Romans 5:2, NIV, adapted*

DECEMBER 8

True Christians do not know vengeance,
no matter how they are mistreated. In
patience they possess their souls.
—*Menno Simons*

Rejoice in hope,
  be patient in suffering,
    persevere in prayer.
—*Romans 12:12, NRSV*

FEBRUARY 6

Peace, which passeth understanding,
Joy, the world can never give,
Now in Jesus I am finding;
In his smiles of love I live.
—*Mary D. James*

Grace to you and peace from God our Father
and the Lord Jesus Christ.
—*Philemon 1:3, NRSV*

DECEMBER 7

It is not surprising that the world is violent beyond belief; but it is to the shame of the church that Christians have participated in and escalated the violence.
—*Duane Beachy*

Let us therefore make every effort to do what leads to peace and to mutual edification.
—*Romans 14:19, NIV*

FEBRUARY 7

Our purpose is not to do away with all quarrels among the children. . . . Our job seems to be . . . to provide them creative ways to get out of the holes they dig for themselves. The best present I know to give a child is a good shovel.

—*Linda Crawford, 1989-94 Director of Prairie Creek Community School, committed to peace education and new ways of teaching*

Pride only breeds quarrels,
    but wisdom is found in those who take advice.
—*Proverbs 13:10, NIV*

DECEMBER 6

Whereas peacemaking in general may seem
so vast as to be unattainable, relating peace
to justice opens the door to every individual
and every group to let peacemaking be part
of what is done every day and in every way.
—*Robert McAfee Brown*

In the same way, faith by itself,
if it is not accompanied by action,
is dead.
—*James 2:17, NIV*

FEBRUARY 8

Dialogue is more than your giving me space to say my words, and my giving you space to say yours. It involves our listening. We are all very different. We cannot have dialogue unless we honor the differences.
—*Elizabeth O'Connor*

Speaking the truth in love, we must grow up in every way into him who is the head, into Christ.
—*Ephesians 4:15, NRSV*

DECEMBER 5

There has never been a war yet which, if
the facts had been put calmly before the
ordinary folk, could not have been prevented.
The common man is the greatest protection against war.
—*Ernest Bevin, speech, House of Commons, November 1945*

Speak tenderly to Jerusalem,
   and cry to her
that she has served her term,
   that her penalty is paid,
that she has received from the Lord's hand
   double for all her sins.
—*Isaiah 40:2, NRSV*

FEBRUARY 9

Nonviolence is the constant awareness
of the dignity and humanity of oneself
and others; it seeks truth and justice; it renounces violence both
in method and in attitude. . . . It is the willingness to undergo
suffering rather than inflict it. It excludes retaliation and flight.
—*Wally Nelson, conscientious objector and tax resister*

To this you were called, because Christ suffered for you, leaving
you an example, that you should follow in his steps.
—*1 Peter 2:21, NIV*

DECEMBER 4

I can't say what it takes to bring peace to the whole world, but I have a feeling that it has to do with each and every individual committing themselves to the way of peace, to loving others, to giving to others, to maybe sacrificing some of our own agenda for the sake of being in right relationship with God and with our neighbor.

—*Mike Chandler*

Let justice roll down like waters,
and righteousness like an everflowing stream.

—*Amos 5:24, NRSV*

FEBRUARY 10

Peace. The choice of a new generation.
—*Matt Bell, seventh-grader*

The Lord is good;
   his steadfast love endures forever,
   and his faithfulness to all generations.
—*Psalm 100:5, NRSV*

Our Father knows that our rest is found
only in receiving a sense of well-being that,
no matter our circumstances, is like the
sense one has after a gallop on horseback
or a plunge in a forest pool or the glorious sea.
—*Amy Carmichael*

For Christ himself is our peace, who has made the two one and
has destroyed the barrier, the dividing wall of hostility.
—*Ephesians 2:14, NIV, adapted*

FEBRUARY 11

All the great military geniuses of the world, Alexander, Julius Caesar, Napoleon, have talked about peace as a distant goal, an end they sought. We must think of peace not only as a goal, but as the means to that goal.
—*Martin Luther King Jr.*

There is no peace," says the Lord, "for the wicked."
—*Isaiah 48:22, NIV*

DECEMBER 2

It is not what happens to us in any day that
gives content to our lives, but whether or
not we let its experience sink into us.
—*Elizabeth O'Connor*

Their delight is in the law of the Lord,
  and on his law they meditate day and night.
They are like trees planted by streams of water,
  which yield their fruit in its season,
    and their leaves do not wither.
—*Psalm 1:2-3, NRSV*

FEBRUARY 12

Don't ever let them pull you down so low
as to hate them.
—*Booker T. Washington*

Whoever says, "I am in the light," while hating a brother
or sister, is still in the darkness.
—*1 John 2:9, NRSV*

DECEMBER 1

There is something good in everything. . . .
But loving the partial goodness in others,
we bring them more quickly to the circle
of Goodness which is God.
—*Fulton John Sheen*

Whoever loves a brother or sister lives in the light, and in such
a person there is no cause for stumbling.
—*1 John 2:10, NRSV*

FEBRUARY 13

A "peacemaker" actively promotes peace and understanding, and works for what is the basis of any real peace—justice, equality, brotherhood, and at the deepest level, peace with God.

—*Duane Beachy*

Let us then pursue what makes for peace and for mutual upbuilding.

—*Romans 14:19, NRSV*

NOVEMBER 30

The whole Scripture speaks of mercifulness
and love, and it is the only sign whereby
a true Christian may be known.
—*Menno Simons*

We know love by this, that he laid down his life for us—
and we ought to lay down our lives for one another.
—*1 John 3:16, NRSV*

FEBRUARY 14
St. Valentine's Day

An act of love may tip the balance.
—*Elie Wiesel*

Happy are those who find wisdom,
    and those who get understanding. . . .
Her ways are ways of pleasantness,
    and all her paths are peace.
—*Proverbs 3:13, 17, NRSV*

NOVEMBER 29

Whatever enhances the well-being
of the human family is peacemaking,
the spreading of shalom.
—*Robert McAfee Brown*

What does the Lord require of you
  but to do justice,
  and to love kindness,
  and to walk humbly with your God?
—*Micah 6:8, NRSV*

FEBRUARY 15

A pacifist believes that there is always an alternative to war.

—*Jeannette Rankin, the lone U.S. Congress member who voted against entering World War II*

My salvation and my honor depend on God; he is my mighty rock, my refuge.

—*Psalm 62:7, NIV*

NOVEMBER 28

Every gun that is made, every warship
launched, every rocket fired, signifies,
in the final sense, a theft from those who
hunger and are not fed, those who are cold
and are not clothed.
—*Dwight D. Eisenhower, April 1953*

Blessed are those who hunger and thirst for righteousness,
  for they will be filled.
—*Matthew 5:6, NRSV*

FEBRUARY 16

The real patriot is the person who is not afraid to criticize the defective policies of the country which he loves. He never belittles or disdains the affection of others for their native lands. Our common humanity is more basic than any political distinctions.
—*Joseph J. Fahey*

Love one another with mutual affection;
outdo one another in showing honor.
—*Romans 12:10, NRSV*

NOVEMBER 27

Say not you know another entirely, till you
have divided an inheritance with him.
—*Johann Kaspar Lavater*

If it is possible, as far as it depends on you,
live peaceably with all.
—*Romans 12:18, NRSV*

FEBRUARY 17

This statement may not be profound, but it is accurate: ignorance breeds distrust. We cannot love what we do not know.
—*Joseph Allegretti, Professor of Law*

There is no fear in love. But perfect love drives out fear, because fear has to do with punishment. The one who fears is not made perfect in love.
—*1 John 4:18, NIV*

NOVEMBER 26

As you come to know the seriousness of our situation—the war, the racism, the poverty in the world—you come to realize it is not going to be changed just by words or demonstrations. It's a question of risking your life. It's a question of living your life in drastically different ways.

—*Dorothy Day*

Be blameless and innocent, children of God without blemish in the midst of a crooked and perverse generation, in which you shine like stars in the world.

—*Philippians 2:15, NRSV*

FEBRUARY 18

The peacemaker . . . knows that true peace
can only emerge when justice is done. So
he works for justice.
—*Culbert G. Rutenber*

Thus says the Lord:
    Act with justice and righteousness,
    and deliver from the hand of the oppressor
        anyone who has been robbed.
—*Jeremiah 22:3, NRSV*

NOVEMBER 25

If we do not trust in God to save us from our enemies, we become idolaters.
—*Lois Barrett*

My soul finds rest in God alone;
    my salvation comes from him.
He alone is my rock and my salvation.
—*Psalm 62:1-2a, NIV*

FEBRUARY 19

Every believer in this world of ours must be a spark of light, a center of love, a vivifying leaven. This is the peace which we implore of him with the ardent yearning of our every prayer.

—*Pope John XXIII*

The God who said, "Let light shine out of darkness," . . . has shone in our hearts to give the light of the knowledge of the glory of God in the face of Jesus Christ.

—*2 Corinthians 4:6, NRSV*

NOVEMBER 24

You give but little when you give of your
possessions. It is when you give of yourself
that you truly give.
—*Kahlil Gibran*

From everyone to whom much has been given,
much will be required;
and from the one to whom much has been entrusted,
even more will be demanded.
—*Luke 12:48b, NRSV*

FEBRUARY 20

Pax Christi, the peace of Christ, is different from the Pax Romana. It is built not on militarism but on justice. There is no other way truly to have peace. We have to choose which kind of peace we will seek and work for.

—*Dorothee Soelle*

The Lord loves justice;
   he will not forsake his faithful ones.
The righteous shall be kept safe forever,
   but the children of the wicked shall be cut off.

—*Psalm 37:28, NRSV*

NOVEMBER 23

I bind my soul this day,
   to the brother far away,
And the sister near at hand,
   in this town, and in this land.
—*Lauchlan MacLean Watt*

A new command I give you:
Love one another. As I have loved you,
so you must love one another.
—*John 13:34, NIV*

FEBRUARY 21

Peace is an activity of cultivating the
process of agreeing—the agreeing that
enables us to continue to work together
cultivating the process of agreeing.
—*Gray Cox*

When you are offering your gift at the altar, if you remember
that your brother or sister has something against you, leave
your gift there before the altar and go; first be reconciled
to your brother or sister.
—*Matthew 5:23-24, NRSV*

NOVEMBER 22

It isn't enough to talk about peace. One must believe in it. And it isn't enough to believe in it. One must work at it.
—*Eleanor Roosevelt*

Be very careful to keep the commandment and the law that Moses the servant of the Lord gave you: to love the Lord your God, to walk in all his ways, to obey his commands, to hold fast to him and to serve him with all your heart and all your soul.
—*Joshua 22:5, NIV*

FEBRUARY 22

If you can live your faith, it is too small.
—*Myron Augsburger*

The apostles said to the Lord, "Increase our faith!" He replied,
"If you have faith as small as a mustard seed, you can say to
this mulberry tree, 'Be uprooted and planted in the sea,' and
it will obey you."
—*Luke 17:5-6, NIV*

NOVEMBER 21

Nonresistants do not have smug and neat solutions for all the complex questions of internal tensions and international relations. For that reason they need to be humble.
—*J. C. Wenger*

Therefore, as God's chosen people, holy and dearly loved, clothe yourselves with compassion, kindness, humility, gentleness and patience.
—*Colossians 3:12, NIV*

FEBRUARY 23

We pray for peace every Sunday at church. Everybody at church prays for peace. Even the people who are sleeping.
—*Eric, age 9*

Then Jesus returned to his disciples and found them sleeping. "Simon," he said to Peter, "are you asleep? Could you not keep watch for one hour?"
—*Mark 14:37, NIV, adapted*

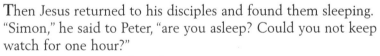

NOVEMBER 20

I'm not trying to change the world. I'm trying to keep the world from changing me.
—*Ammon Hennacy*

Take no part in the unfruitful works of darkness, but instead expose them.
—*Ephesians 5:11, NRSV*

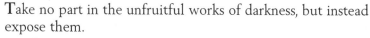

FEBRUARY 24

In prayerful solitude I find not only God
and myself but the world and all in it, not
as it sees itself but as it stands in reality.
—*Robert Faricy, S.J.*

Sow for yourselves righteousness,
   reap the fruit of unfailing love,
and break up your unplowed ground;
   for it is time to seek the Lord,
until he comes and showers righteousness on you.
—*Hosea 10:12, NIV*

NOVEMBER 19

Action is the great need of the Eastern
World; silence the need of the Western.
—*Fulton John Sheen*

I have stilled and quieted my soul;
   like a weaned child with its mother,
   like a weaned child is my soul within me.
—*Psalm 131:2, NIV*

FEBRUARY 25

The hour has come for educators, sociologists, and citizens to reverse their steps, to see that if the self is to be really happy, it must be disciplined, pruned, denied, and negated by itself.
—*Fulton John Sheen*

All of us make many mistakes. Anyone who makes no mistakes in speaking is perfect, able to keep the whole body in check with a bridle.
—*James 3:2, NRSV*

NOVEMBER 18

The whole life of our Savior was given over to the practice of nonresistance, . . . which was brought to life in the Anabaptist movement. From time to time in the history of the Christian church, [nonresistance] has been emphasized, and always the church has been strengthened and come to new life because of it.

—*Richard Bentzinger, United Methodist minister, speech to Civilian Public Service reunion*

Jesus said, "Father, forgive them; for they do not know what they are doing." And they cast lots to divide his clothing.
—*Luke 23:34, NRSV*

FEBRUARY 26

When I love someone, I seek what is best
for them.
—*Billy Graham*

My command is this: Love each other as I have loved you.
—*Jesus, in John 15:12, NIV*

NOVEMBER 17

The most wasted day of all is that on which we have not laughed.
—*Sebastien R. N. Chamfort*

A happy heart makes the face cheerful,
   but heartache crushes the spirit.
—*Proverbs 15:13, NIV*

FEBRUARY 27

It is my conviction that one cannot really understand or know what Jesus was saying and doing without understanding that it was done in the context of nonresistance.

—*Richard Bentzinger, United Methodist minister,
at a Civilian Public Service reunion*

Through Christ, God was pleased to reconcile to himself all things, whether on earth or in heaven, by making peace through the blood of his cross.

—*Colossians 1:20, NRSV, adapted*

NOVEMBER 16

As I meditate on and study Scripture, as I spend time in prayer, then I become aware of God's grace toward me and toward the world as a whole. . . . I can tell when I have not spent time in prayer because my reactions . . . are not as loving, not as peaceful, not as hopeful.
—*Mike Chandler*

Great peace have those who love your law;
  nothing can make them stumble.
—*Psalm 119:165, NRSV*

FEBRUARY 28

To be great is to be misunderstood.
—*Ralph Waldo Emerson*

They are from the world and therefore speak from the viewpoint of the world, and the world listens to them. We are from God, and whoever knows God listens to us; but whoever is not from God does not listen to us.
—*1 John 4:5-6a, NIV*

NOVEMBER 15

How can I build a bridge across the gulf between me and you unless I am aware of the gulf? How can I communicate with you unless I see how things look from your side?
—*Elizabeth O'Connor*

By the open statement of truth we commend ourselves to the conscience of everyone in the sight of God.
—*2 Corinthians 4:2b, NRSV*

FEBRUARY 29

Peacemaking with children can be a sobering and enlightening journey that brings adults face-to-face with their own prejudices, stereotypes, and power games. The journey can . . . allow [adults] to learn from the child as the child learns from them.
—*Cynthia J. Carney*

Train children in the right way,
  and when old, they will not stray.
—*Proverbs 22:6, NRSV*

NOVEMBER 14

The greatest heroes of the world are not
men who kill other men in war. They are
quiet heroes who are brave in other ways.
—*Rufus Jones, Quaker thinker*

This is what the Sovereign Lord, the Holy One of Israel, says:
  "In repentance and rest is your salvation,
    in quietness and trust is your strength,
    but you would have none of it."
—*Isaiah 30:15, NIV*

MARCH 1

If there were no greed, there would be no occasion for armaments.
—*Mohandas K. Gandhi*

You desire truth in the inward being;
therefore teach me wisdom in my secret heart. . . .
Create in me a clean heart, O God,
and put a new and right spirit within me.
—*Psalm 51:6, 10, NRSV*

NOVEMBER 13

Jesus' way of love implies, therefore, courage to suffer persecution without resistance and retaliation, . . . a tolerant and charitable attitude toward our enemies, and nonresistance to evil. To be able to suffer and to sacrifice is the quintessence of Jesus' way of love.

—*Pyarelal Malagar, Mennonite leader, India*

Do not be astonished, brothers and sisters, that the world hates you.

—*1 John 3:13, NRSV*

MARCH 2

The spirit of Christianity is not narrowly
nationalistic, but universally inclusive.
—*Harry Emerson Fosdick, in a sermon at the
League of Nations Assembly Service, 1925*

Even the nations are like a drop from a bucket,
    and are accounted as dust on the scales;
see, the Lord takes up the isles like fine dust.
—*Isaiah 40:15, NRSV, adapted*

NOVEMBER 12

Being a peace maker, [Jesus] stirred things up like crazy, living his life in a running battle with the Establishment until his enemies nailed him—. . . a tough price to pay for being a reconciler.
—*Culbert G. Rutenber*

I am convinced that neither death, nor life, nor angels, nor rulers, nor things present, nor things to come, nor powers, nor height, nor depth, nor anything else in all creation, will be able to separate us from the love of God in Christ Jesus our Lord.
—*Romans 8:38-39, NRSV*

MARCH 3

Internationalism does not mean the end of individual nations. Orchestras don't mean the end of violins.
—*Golda Meir*

I am coming to gather all nations and tongues; and they shall come and shall see my glory.
—*The Lord, in Isaiah 66:18b, NRSV*

NOVEMBER 11

Many people have observed how, for some
. . . middle-aged males, especially, World War
II was the last great excitement of their life.
Peace is pale by comparison. But we have a biblical concept of
peace that is exactly the opposite. It is full of content, full of life.
—*Gerald O. Pedersen*

You shall go out in joy,
   and be led back in peace;
the mountains and the hills before you
   shall burst into song,
and all the trees of the field shall clap their hands.
—*Isaiah 55:12, NRSV*

MARCH 4

The peace keeper thinks that love is being nice to everyone; the peace maker thinks that love is doing right by everyone.
—*Culbert G. Rutenber*

Be imitators of God, therefore, as dearly loved children and live a life of love, just as Christ loved us and gave himself up for us as a fragrant offering and sacrifice to God.
—*Ephesians 5:1-2, NIV*

NOVEMBER 10

Pleasure comes from without, but joy comes from within, and it is, therefore, within the reach of everyone in the world.
—*Fulton John Sheen*

So do not worry, saying, "What shall we eat?" or "What shall we drink?" or "What shall we wear?"
—*Matthew 6:31, NIV*

MARCH 5

Laity and clergy alike have already noticed how Christians everywhere are rediscovering their calling as peacemakers. Whether marching in New York City or praying in St. Peter's Square, Christians too are crying, "Enough!"

—*Ron J. Sider and Darrel Brubaker*

Jesus Christ came and proclaimed peace to you who were far off and peace to those who were near.

—*Ephesians 2:17, NRSV, adapted*

NOVEMBER 9

If you want peace, work for justice.
—*Pope John XXIII*

Those who oppress the poor insult their Maker,
but those who are kind to the needy honor him.
—*Proverbs 14:31, NRSV*

MARCH 6

It is possible to describe the entire ministry of Jesus as a single act of peacemaking: . . . healing of the sick, the feeding of the hungry, the care of the neglected and despised, and the forgiveness of sins—[these] are all aspects of the restoration of God's peace. . . . The core is captured in the phrase: Jesus the peacemaker.
—*Ulrich Mauser*

The Spirit of the Lord is on me,
  because he has anointed me to preach good news to the poor.
He has sent me to proclaim freedom for the prisoners
  and recovery of sight for the blind, to release the oppressed.
—*Jesus, in Luke 4:18, NIV*

NOVEMBER 8

Peacemaking isn't something we ought to
do in our spare time; it's something we
need to do all the time.
—*Robert McAfee Brown*

One thing God has spoken,
　two things have I heard:
that you, O God, are strong,
　and that you, O Lord, are loving.
—*Psalm 62:11-12a, NIV*

MARCH 7

If world peace is really to come, it's going to be through the efforts of nonpacifists in vast numbers joining with the pacifists.
—*Charles P. Lutz*

God is a God not of disorder but of peace.
—*1 Corinthians 14:33a, NRSV*

NOVEMBER 7

Peace grows out of love.
—*Christian Burkholder*

Blessed are they whose ways are blameless,
   who walk according to the law of the Lord.
—*Psalm 119:1, NIV*

MARCH 8

It is the nature of a prophet that he rarely experiences the fulfillment of his goals in his own time. Rather, his words of warning and insight burn deeply into the collective conscience of his society, from whence they may rise as moral guides for later, better-prepared, and more-receptive generations.

—*Charles DeBenedetti, about* Peace Heroes

Jesus said to them, "Only in his hometown and in his own house is a prophet without honor."

—*Matthew 13:57b, NIV*

NOVEMBER 6

There can be no vulnerability without risk; there can be no community without vulnerability; there can be no peace—and ultimately no life—without community.
—*M. Scott Peck*

Let love be genuine.
—*Romans 12:9a, NRSV*

MARCH 9

Prayer is the key of the morning and
the bolt of the evening.
—*Mohandas K. Gandhi*

Trust in the Lord for ever,
   for in the Lord God
   you have an everlasting rock.
—*Isaiah 26:4, NRSV*

NOVEMBER 5

I have a dream that some day soon, the ingenuity and imagination we [humans] have always prized in our most creative citizens will be turned from the works of war to the inventions of peace.
—*Alan Geyer*

They shall beat their swords into plowshares, and their spears into pruning hooks.
—*Isaiah 2:4, NRSV*

MARCH 10

When peace, like a river, attendeth my way,
When sorrows like sea billows roll,
Whatever my lot,
Thou has taught me to say,
It is well, it is well with my soul.
—*Horatio G. Spafford*

Now may the Lord of peace himself
give you peace at all times and in every way.
The Lord be with all of you.
—*2 Thessalonians 3:16, NIV*

NOVEMBER 4

A lantern shows only the next step—not several steps ahead. . . . If only the next step is clear, the one thing to do is take it!
—*Amy Carmichael*

If any of you is lacking in wisdom, ask God, who gives to all generously and ungrudgingly, and it will be given you.
—*James 1:5, NRSV*

MARCH 11

We have an idea of being peaceable, with everyone getting along. So we may avoid conflict. We may then actually find devious ways to express our resistance to someone else.
—*Ted Grimsrud*

I pray that out of his glorious riches he may strengthen you with power through his Spirit in your inner being.
—*Ephesians 3:16, NIV*

NOVEMBER 3

Pacifism is a reasonable and moral point of view. It does not contend that struggle and conflict can be, or should be, ended. It does argue for the elimination of violence and force as a means of solution.

—*Jeannette Rankin, the lone U.S. Congress member who voted against entering World War II*

Justice will dwell in the desert
    and righteousness live in the fertile field.
—*Isaiah 32:16, NIV*

MARCH 12

The first thing to be disrupted by our commitment to nonviolence will be not the system but our own lives.
—*Jim Douglass*

Jesus said, "Foxes have dens and birds have nests, but I, the Messiah, have no home of my own—no place to lay my head."
—*Matthew 8:20, LB*

NOVEMBER 2

The New Testament teaches us that there is only one God, and that all of us are children of that one God. This is the basic theology of peace. It is taught by all the great religions of the world. It is so simple that a child can understand it.
—*Richard McSorley*

Yet to all who received him, to those who believed in his name, he gave the right to become children of God.
—*John 1:12, NIV, speaking of the true light, Christ*

MARCH 13

Over the years we have gone on piling weapon upon weapon, missile upon missile, almost involuntarily, like lemmings heading for the sea.... We have to break out of the circle; we have no other choice.
—*George F. Kennan, winner of the 1981 Albert Einstein Peace Prize*

I say to you, Do not resist an evildoer. But if anyone strikes you on the right cheek, turn the other also.
—*Jesus, in Matthew 5:39, NRSV*

NOVEMBER 1

Let there be light, Lord God of Hosts!
Let there be wisdom on the earth!
Let broad humanity have birth!
Let there be deeds, instead of boasts.
—*William Merrell Vories*

In the king's days may righteousness flourish
    and peace abound, until the moon is no more.
—*Psalm 72:7, NRSV, adapted*

MARCH 14

Jesus asks us to speak for peace whether or not it is effective in the worldly sense. The whole question is the question of faithfulness and not just the question of change. . . . So in the middle of this world we need to say "no" to war even when we don't see immediate results.

—*Henri Nouwen*

Hold . . . on to faith and a good conscience. Some have rejected these and so have shipwrecked their faith.

—*1 Timothy 1:19, NIV*

OCTOBER 31

It is other folks' dogs and children that make most of the bad feelings between neighbors.
—*Ellis Parker Butler*

You shall not hate in your heart anyone of your kin.
—*Leviticus 19:17a, NRSV*

MARCH 15

It is not only Christians but all just people
who must refuse to become soldiers.
—*Leo Tolstoy, giving "Advice to a Draftee"*

As for God, his way is perfect;
   the word of the Lord is flawless.
He is a shield for all who take refuge in him.
—*Psalm 18:30, NIV*

OCTOBER 30

You can't shake hands with a clenched fist.
—*Indira Gandhi*

Now you must rid yourselves of all such things as these: anger, rage, malice, slander and filthy language from your lips.
—*Colossians 3:8, NIV*

MARCH 16

The more I become identified with God,
the more will I be identified with all the
others who are identified with him.
—*Thomas Merton*

The children of God and the children of the devil are revealed
in this way: all who do not do what is right are not from God,
nor are those who do not love their brothers and sisters.
—*1 John 3:10, NRSV*

OCTOBER 29

It is harder to work for peace than to drift
into war.
—*Joseph J. Fahey*

Do not be overcome by evil,
   but overcome evil with good.
—*Romans 12:21, NRSV*

MARCH 17

Violence is not something that happens only at gunpoint. It is present whenever the human dignity of an individual is oppressed, ignored, or abused.
—*Ronald C. Arnett*

Happy are those whose help is the God of Jacob,
    whose hope is in the Lord their God,
who made heaven and earth, the sea, and all that is in them;
who keeps faith forever;
    who executes justice for the oppressed;
who gives food to the hungry.
The Lord sets the prisoners free.
—*Psalm 146:5-7, NIV*

OCTOBER 28

Active love is the response Jesus wants us to have even toward our enemies. Our love is to be independent of the attitude of the other person. We are to love simply because God wants us to reveal ourselves as true sons and daughters of our heavenly parent by this love.
—*Richard McSorley*

If you love those who love you,
   what reward do you have?
Do not even the tax collectors do the same?
—*Matthew 5:46, NRSV*

MARCH 18

We are witnessing the beginnings of a conversion in the churches—a conversion to peace. The signs of it are everywhere. . . . Where the commitment to peace is emerging, so is Bible study, prayer, the renewal of worship, and community.
—*Jim Wallis*

We know that all things work together for good for those who love God, who are called according to his purpose.
—*Romans 8:28, NRSV*

OCTOBER 27

A global system which outlaws war and provides for a lawful appraisal of contested claims is, in principle, just as feasible as the legal devices which restrain and provide alternatives to violence within the nation-states.

—*Ralph L. Moellering*

Teach them the decrees and laws, and show them the way to live. . . . Have them serve as judges for the people.

—*Exodus 18:20a, 22a, NIV*

MARCH 19

When I go to an evangelism academy, I see
very few people that I would also see at a
peacemaking conference, and vice versa.
This is a real tragedy.

—*Bob Hull, General Conference Mennonite Church*
  Peace and Justice Secretary

Make every effort to keep the unity of the Spirit through
the bond of peace.

—*Ephesians 4:3, NIV*

OCTOBER 26

The pacifist thinks there is only one tribe.
Billions of members. They come first. We
think killing any member of the family is a dumb idea.
—*Joan Baez*

You have heard that it was said to the people long ago, "Do not
murder, and anyone who murders will be subject to judgment."
—*Matthew 5:21, NIV*

MARCH 20

We must love the jailer as well as the one
in prison. We must do that seemingly utterly
impossible thing: love our enemy.
—*Dorothy Day*

For nothing is impossible with God.
—*Luke 1:37, NIV*

OCTOBER 25

Instead of hating the people you think are
war makers, hate the appetites and the
disorder in your own soul, which are the
causes of war.
—*Thomas Merton*

If you harbor bitter envy and selfish ambition in your hearts,
do not boast about it or deny the truth.
—*James 3:14, NIV*

MARCH 21

This generation has, quite humbly, the final responsibility and the last chance to turn terror into hope.
—*Albert Einstein*

The Lord said to Gideon, "Peace be to you; do not fear, you shall not die."
—*Judges 6:23, NRSV, adapted*

OCTOBER 24

Peace is our work. . . . To everyone, Christians, believers, and men and women of good will, I say: Do not be afraid to take a chance on peace, to teach peace. . . . Peace will be the last word of history.
—*Pope John Paul II*

In all these things we are more than conquerors through Christ, who loved us.
—*Romans 8:37, NRSV, adapted*

MARCH 22

Peace is never just the result of human effort, and never practical in the sense of being done by human power alone.
—*Richard McSorley*

The Lord gives strength to his people;
the Lord blesses his people with peace.
—*Psalm 29:11, NIV*

OCTOBER 23

Joy is the most infallible sign of the
presence of God.
—*Leon Bloy*

A cheerful heart is good medicine,
   but a crushed spirit dries up the bones.
—*Proverbs 17:22, NIV*

MARCH 23

The Eastern World has struck on the secret
of inner peace by suggesting that inner
happiness is dependent on the control
and limitation of desires.
—*Fulton John Sheen*

I have learned to be content with whatever I have.
—*Paul, in Philippians 4:11, NRSV*

OCTOBER 22

Peacemaking is fundamentally a spiritual
struggle, a battle for the soul of humanity.
—*Richard Barnet, a founder of World Peacemakers*

God will redeem my soul from the grave.
—*Psalm 49:15a, NIV*

MARCH 24

Suffering and death may be part of the
legacy for those who seek peace and pursue
it as he did.
—*Gerald O. Pedersen, referring to Christ*

It has been granted to you on behalf of Christ
not only to believe on him, but also to suffer
for him.
—*Philippians 1:29, NIV*

OCTOBER 21

We shall never truly know ourselves unless we find people who can listen, who can enable us to emerge, to come out of ourselves, to discover who we are. We cannot discover ourselves by ourselves.
—*Edward Farrell*

Oh, that I had one to hear me!
   (Here is my signature! let the Almighty answer me!)
   Oh, that I had the indictment written by my adversary!
—*Job 31:35, NRSV*

MARCH 25

The pacifism of Jesus . . . is never
"passivism."
—*G. H. C. Macgregor*

Do not suppose that I have come to bring peace to the earth.
I did not come to bring peace, but a sword.
—*Jesus, in Matthew 10:34, NIV*

OCTOBER 20

Wherever the Prince of Peace goes before us with his love in our whole world we need to awaken, inform, and activate people—and whatever the obstacles, never be deterred! This is the aggressive pursuit of peace.
—*Gerald O. Pedersen*

If God is for us, who can be against us?
—*Romans 8:31, NIV*

MARCH 26

Peace is waking up in the morning and the only news is sports.
—*Kevin, age 8*

The quiet words of the wise are more to be heeded than the shouts of a ruler of fools.
—*Ecclesiastes 9:17, NIV*

OCTOBER 19

We believe that the church is God's "holy nation" . . . and needs no violence for its protection. . . . As Christians we are to respect those in authority and to pray for all people, including those in government. . . . [We call] the nations (and all persons and institutions) to move toward justice, peace, and compassion for all people. In so doing, we seek the welfare of the city to which God has sent us.
—*Confession of Faith in a Mennonite Perspective*

For lack of guidance a nation falls,
    but many advisers make victory sure.
—*Proverbs 11:14, NIV*

MARCH 27

Dueling, slavery, and ritual human sacrifice are all human institutions which have been dispensed with by law due to a crystallized public opinion. The war method of settling disputes can be dispensed with in the same way simply by the decision to eliminate it from the lexicon of acceptable alternatives.

—*Jeannette Rankin, the lone U.S. Congress member who voted against entering World War II*

Where there is envy and selfish ambition, there will also be disorder and wickedness of every kind.

—*James 3:16, NRSV*

OCTOBER 18

Somehow it was instilled in me that the only cause worth dying for was the cause of Christ, not one's country.
—*Melodie M. Davis*

I lay down my life for the sheep.
—*Jesus, in John 10:15b, NIV*

MARCH 28

Christ won't kill. I won't either.
—*Bill Wilkins, U.S. Army Private, speaking to the head commander on his base, 1966*

Pursue peace with everyone, and the holiness without which no one will see the Lord.
—*Hebrews 12:14, NRSV*

OCTOBER 17

The apostle Peter says we pastors must be examples to our flocks. We pastors must teach about forgiveness. Then we can help resolve many conflicts among church members. It is also important that we live with the spirit of humility and forgiveness.

—*Kusangila Kitondo, Mennonite leader, Zaire*

I have set you an example that you should do as I have done for you.

—*John 13:15, NIV*

MARCH 29

The God of peace is never glorified
by human violence.
—*Thomas Merton*

To set the mind on the flesh is death, but to set the mind
on the Spirit is life and peace.
—*Romans 8:6, NRSV*

OCTOBER 16

It is useless to dream of reforming socio-economic structures . . . without a corresponding deep change in our inner lives.
—*Archbishop Dom Helder Camara*

Since we are justified by faith, we have peace with God through our Lord Jesus Christ.
—*Romans 5:1, NRSV*

MARCH 30

There are two ways to get enough. One is
to continue to accumulate more and more.
The other is to desire less.
—*G. K. Chesterton*

Each of you must give as you have made up your mind,
not reluctantly or under compulsion, for God loves
a cheerful giver.
—*2 Corinthians 9:7, NRSV*

OCTOBER 15

We need peace more than we need
pacifism. We need peacebuilders more than
we need pacifists.
—*Charles P. Lutz*

The people who walked in darkness
   have seen a great light;
those who lived in a land of deep darkness—
   on them light has shined.
—*Isaiah 9:2, NRSV*

MARCH 31

It is of the very nature of peace to permit different people to do different things towards its establishment, to stress different ways of making it real, to honor a variety of gifts in the service of a common objective.
—*Edward Leroy Long Jr.*

There are varieties of gifts, but the same Spirit; and there are varieties of services, but the same Lord; and there are varieties of activities, but it is the same God who activates all of them in everyone.
—*1 Corinthians 12:4-6, NRSV*

OCTOBER 14

Peace is a time for love.
—*Doreen, age 7*

There is a time for everything,
and a season for every activity under heaven.
—*Ecclesiastes 3:1, NIV*

APRIL 1

It will be a great day when our schools get all the money they need and the air force has to hold a bake sale to buy a bomber.

—*Women's International League for Peace and Freedom*

Every valley shall be raised up,
  every mountain and hill made low;
the rough ground shall become level,
  the rugged places a plain.

—*Isaiah 40:4, NIV*

OCTOBER 13

How shall a Christian wage war? Nay, how shall he even be a soldier in peacetime without the sword, which the Lord had taken away, . . . the Lord, . . . in disarming Peter, ungirded every soldier.
—*Tertullian, early church leader, 160-220*

Jesus said to him, "Put your sword back into its place."
—*Jesus, in Matthew 26:52a, NRSV*

APRIL 2

We are not called to change the world. We are called to live truly changed lives and to proclaim to the world the transforming love of Jesus Christ.
—*Duane Beachy*

Clothe yourselves with the new self, created according to the likeness of God in true righteousness and holiness.
—*Ephesians 4:24, NRSV*

OCTOBER 12

Let woe and waste of warfare cease,
That useful labor yet may build
Its homes with love and virtue filled!
God, give thy wayward children peace!
—*William Merrell Vories*

Peace be within your walls,
     and security within your towers.
—*Psalm 122:7, NRSV*

APRIL 3

God has no one but us to do the very things
we ask him for.
—*Louis Evely*

Do not merely listen to the word, and so deceive yourselves.
Do what it says.
—*James 1:22, NIV*

OCTOBER 11

A modest proposal for peace: let the Christians of the world agree that they will not kill each other.
—*John Stoner, MCC poster*

Be at peace with each other.
—*Mark 9:50b, NIV*

APRIL 4

I believe without a shadow of doubt that science and peace will finally triumph over ignorance and war, and that the nations of earth will ultimately agree not to destroy, but to build up.

—*Louis Pasteur*

The Lord bless you and keep you;
the Lord make his face to shine upon you,
   and be gracious to you;
The Lord lift up his countenance upon you,
   and give you peace.

—*Numbers 6:24-26, NRSV*

OCTOBER 10

The things, good Lord, that we pray for,
give us the grace to labor for.
—*Sir Thomas More*

Praise the Lord!
   Happy are those who fear the Lord,
   who greatly delight in his commandments.
—*Psalm 112:1, NRSV*

APRIL 5

God can only be comprehended by love,
not by our intellect.
—*Anonymous English monk*, The Cloud of Unknowing

Put things in order, listen to my appeal, agree with one another,
live in peace; and the God of love and peace will be with you.
—*2 Corinthians 13:11b, NRSV*

OCTOBER 9

It's easier for a child in North America to find a gun than to find a good book, a good friend, a good school, or a good minister.
—*Jack Dueck, storyteller and consultant*

Listen! the valiant cry in the streets;
    the envoys of peace weep bitterly.
—*Isaiah 33:7, NRSV*

APRIL 6

Let there be peace on earth,
    and let it begin with me.
—*Sy Miller and Jill Jackson, in a folk hymn*

Peace I leave with you; my peace I give to you. I do not give
to you as the world gives. Do not let your hearts be troubled,
and do not let them be afraid.
—*John 14:27, NRSV*

No longer [are we] concerned with being
Catholic or Protestant or Anabaptist, but
simply faithful disciples of a risen Lord,
who still greets us with his "Peace be with you."
—*Walter Klaassen*

Jesus said to them again, "Peace be with you. As the Father
has sent me, so I send you."
—*John 20:21, NRSV*

APRIL 7

No more war, war never again.
—*Pope Paul VI*

Then those who live in the towns of Israel will go out and use the weapons for fuel and burn them up—the small and large shields, the bows and arrows, the war clubs and spears. For seven years they will use them for fuel.
—*Ezekiel 39:9, NIV*

OCTOBER 7

Action . . . flows from a dream that someday the sons and daughters of communists and Christians will frolic together; Arab as well as North American children will enjoy the earth's fruits; the tanks will be melted into playground equipment; the full glory of God will be revealed, and all flesh, united, will see it.

—*Gene Stoltzfus*

The wolf will live with the lamb,
   the leopard will lie down with the goat,
the calf and the lion and the yearling together;
   and a little child will lead them.

—*Isaiah 11:6, NIV*

APRIL 8

Let us be wary of mass solutions, let us be wary of statistics. We must love our neighbors as ourselves.
—*Father Dominique Pire*

Love does no wrong to a neighbor; therefore, love is the fulfilling of the law.
—*Romans 13:10, NRSV*

OCTOBER 6

Beyond prayer, probably the single most important thing we can do as peacemakers is to make the message of peace and suffering love an integral part of our evangelistic proclamation of the good news of Jesus Christ.

—*Duane Beachy*

In Christ God was reconciling the world to himself, not counting their trespasses against them, and entrusting the message of reconciliation to us.

—*2 Corinthians 5:19, NRSV*

APRIL 9

I do not believe in short-violent-cuts to
success. . . . However much I may
sympathize with and admire worthy motives, I am an
uncompromising opponent of violent methods even to serve
the noblest of causes.
—*Mohandas K. Gandhi*

Happy are those
　who do not follow the advice of the wicked,
or take the path that sinners tread,
　or sit in the seat of scoffers.
—*Psalm 1:1, NRSV*

OCTOBER 5

Listen to others talk. . . . You will probably be amazed to see how often neither side listens actively to the other. . . . When a child communicates, he wants concrete evidence that his message has been received.
—*Dorothy Corkille Briggs*

Jesus called for them and said, "Let the little children come to me, and do not stop them; for it is to such as these that the kingdom of God belongs."
—*Luke 18:16, NRSV*

APRIL 10

We have grasped the mystery of the atom and rejected the Sermon on the Mount. Ours is a world of nuclear giants and ethical infants. We know more about war than we do about peace—more about killing than we do about living.

—*General Omar Bradley*

Bring joy to your servant,
    for to you, O Lord, I lift up my soul.
You are forgiving and good, O Lord,
    abounding in love to all who call to you.

—*Psalm 86:4-5, NIV*

OCTOBER 4

All the good that you will do will come not from you but from the fact that you have allowed yourself, in the obedience of faith, to be used by God's love. Think of this more, and gradually you will be free from the need to prove yourself, and you can be more open to the power that will work through you without your knowing it.
—*Thomas Merton*

Lord, you establish peace for us;
all that we have accomplished
   you have done for us.
—*Isaiah 26:12, NIV*

APRIL 11

Victory can be achieved by various means.
It can be gained with tanks and missiles,
but I think that one wins better with truth, honesty, and logic
. . . . This is a new weapon.
—Lech Walesa, November 1982

The Lord will fight for you,
and you have only to keep still.
—Exodus 14:14, NRSV

OCTOBER 3

There is perhaps no surer road to peace than the one that starts from little islands and oases of genuine kindness, islands and oases constantly growing in number and being continually joined together until eventually they ring the world.

—*Father Dominique Pire*

Jesus also saw a poor widow put in two very small copper coins. "I tell you the truth," he said, "this poor widow has put in more than all the others."

—*Luke 21:2-3, NIV, adapted*

APRIL 12

Caring about the world doesn't begin with fear or morbidity but with fascination.
—*Garrison Keillor*

The heavens declare the glory of God;
   the skies proclaim the work of his hands.
—*Psalm 19:1, NIV*

OCTOBER 2

The great quest for Christians around the world is to break down the walls of hostility that separate us. Our common baptism calls us to learn of one another's cultures, customs, and beliefs, that we may truly celebrate our unity amid our diversity.
—*James G. Kirk*

If you were not to associate with the immoral of this world, or the greedy and robbers, or idolaters—you would then need to go out of the world.
—*1 Corinthians 5:9-10, NRSV, rephrased*

APRIL 13

In comfortable settings, the gospel is often spiritualized to the extent that it helps us avoid responsibility for our neighbor's oppression.
—*Titus Peachey, MCC U.S. Peace and Justice Co-Secretary*

Whoever has two coats must share with anyone who has none; and whoever has food must do likewise.
—*Luke 3:11, NRSV*

OCTOBER 1

Commitment for peace should grow out
of spirituality. My first commitment is
to God and to my relationship to God.
—*Mike Chandler*

We have come to share in Christ if we hold firmly till the end
the confidence we had at first.
—*Hebrews 3:14, NIV*

APRIL 14

Those who work for peace will do best if they keep open the process of exchanging ideas, if they respect the differing commitments of others, and if they give persons of many persuasions love and support.
—*Edward Leroy Long Jr.*

We have gifts that differ according to the grace given to us: prophecy, in proportion to faith; ministry, in ministering; the teacher, in teaching.
—*Romans 12:6-7, NRSV*

SEPTEMBER 30

Join hands, then, people of the faith,
　　whate'er your race may be.
Who serves my Father as a son,
　　is surely kin to me.
—*John Oxenham*

Welcome one another, therefore, just as Christ has welcomed
you, for the glory of God.
—*Romans 15:7, NRSV*

APRIL 15

Another argument in favor of a lasting
peace is that it would give us time to finish
paying for the last war.
—*In* Salt and Pepper

I will appoint Peace as your overseer
 and Righteousness as your taskmaster.
Violence shall no more be heard in your land,
 devastation or destruction within your borders;
you shall call your walls Salvation,
 and your gates Praise.
—*Isaiah 60:17b-18, NRSV*

SEPTEMBER 29

The resurrection assures us that the victory is won already. That is why we can afford the costly way of nonviolence. With Jesus Christ going before us, we walk in the glorious light of his resurrection.
—*Duane Beachy*

If we live, we live to the Lord; and if we die, we die to the Lord. So, whether we live or die, we belong to the Lord.
—*Romans 14:8, NIV*

APRIL 16

Political realists and media commentators cannot imagine a world without nuclear weapons. Only those with the eyes of faith will be able to see it. But if those who do will persevere like their abolitionist forebears, many others will eventually come to see the way to a world free of the nuclear scourge.
—*Jim Wallis*

Now faith is the assurance of things hoped for,
the conviction of things not seen.
—*Hebrews 11:1, NRSV*

SEPTEMBER 28

We should say to each of them: Do you know what you are? You are a marvel. You are unique. In all the world there is no other child exactly like you; . . . and when you grow up, can you then harm another who is, like you, a marvel? You must cherish one another. You must work—we must all work—to make this world worthy of its children.

—*Pablo Casals*

Then Jesus took a little child and put it among them; and taking it in his arms, he said to them, "Whoever welcomes one such child in my name welcomes me, and whoever welcomes me welcomes not me but the one who sent me."

—*Mark 9:36-37, NRSV, adapted*

APRIL 17

I conclude before my God that worldly
power is not needed in the kingdom
of Christ.
—*Pilgram Marpeck, MCC poster*

Yours, O Lord, is the greatness and the power
and the glory and the majesty and splendor,
for everything in heaven and earth is yours.
—*David, praising God, in 1 Chronicles 29:11a, NIV*

SEPTEMBER 27

The pen is mightier than the sword.
—*Edward Robert Bulwer Lytton,*
viceroy of India, 1875-1880

The Lord sent out his word and healed them,
    and delivered them from destruction.
—*Psalm 107:20, NRSV, adapted*

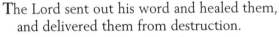

APRIL 18

I am only one, but still I am one. I cannot do everything, but still I can do something; and because I cannot do everything, I will not refuse to do the something that I can do.
—*Edward Everett Hale*

We have not stopped praying for you and asking God to fill you with the knowledge of his will through all spiritual wisdom and understanding. And we pray this in order that you may live a life worthy of the Lord and may please him in every way: bearing fruit in every good work, growing in the knowledge of God.
—*Colossians 1:9b-10, NIV*

SEPTEMBER 26

It is human experience that people who have been forgiven sometimes find in themselves a new capacity to forgive.
—*John Oliver Nelson*

Do not judge, or you too will be judged. For in the same way you judge others, you will be judged, and with the measure you use, it will be measured to you.
—*Matthew 7:1-2, NIV*

APRIL 19

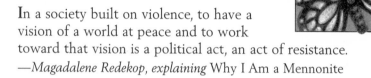

In a society built on violence, to have a
vision of a world at peace and to work
toward that vision is a political act, an act of resistance.
—*Magadalene Redekop, explaining* Why I Am a Mennonite

This is what the Sovereign Lord says: ". . . I will spend my wrath
against . . . those prophets of Israel who prophesied to Jerusalem
and saw visions of peace for her when there was no peace,
declares the Sovereign Lord."
—*Ezekiel 13:13-16, NIV*

SEPTEMBER 25

People who love life have always longed for peace. . . . Millions have died seeking peace. But sadly, eons of longing have produced little more than fear and frustration. . . . If the churches are to be united in a new abolitionist movement, . . . the preachers of our land must issue the summons.
—*Ron J. Sider and Darrel Brubaker*

These are the things you are to do: Speak the truth to each other, and render true and sound judgment in your courts.
—*Zechariah 8:16, NIV*

APRIL 20

Peace is a thing you can't have by throwing rocks at a hornet's nest.
—*In* Salt and Pepper

When you enter a house, first say, "Peace to this house."
—*Luke 10:5, NIV*

SEPTEMBER 24

One day . . . we will make a choice. Either we will sink into the final coma and end it all or, as I trust and believe, we will awaken to the truth of our peril, . . . we will break through the layers of our denials, put aside our fainthearted excuses, and rise up to cleanse the earth of nuclear weapons.
—*Jonathan Schell*

See, I have set before you today life and prosperity, death and adversity. . . . Choose life so that you and your descendants may live.
—*Deuteronomy 30:15, 19, NRSV*

APRIL 21

We work [for peace] as though it all depended on us and trust as though it all depended on God.
—*Culbert G. Rutenber*

As you therefore have received Christ Jesus the Lord, continue to live your lives in him.
—*Colossians 2:6, NRSV*

SEPTEMBER 23

Perhaps those . . . Christians among us who refuse to bear arms for the purpose of shedding human blood, may be preserved by divine providence as the center of a circle, which shall gradually embrace all nations of the earth in a perpetual treaty of friendship and peace.

—*Dr. Benjamin Rush, Philadelphia physician*

Do not repay evil with evil or abuse for abuse; but, on the contrary, repay with a blessing. It is for this that you were called—that you might inherit a blessing.

—*1 Peter 3:9, NRSV*

APRIL 22

Treat the earth well. . . . It was not given
to you by your parents. . . . It was lent
to you by your children.
—*Kenyan proverb*

The earth is the Lord's
  and all that is in it,
the world,
  and those who live in it.
—*Psalm 24:1, NRSV*

SEPTEMBER 22

Give us the peace of vision clear
To see our brothers' good our own,
To joy and suffer not alone:
The love that casteth out all fear!
—*William Merrell Vories*

This is love for God: to obey his commands.
And his commands are not burdensome.
—*1 John 5:3, NIV*

APRIL 23

There is an unmistakable connection
between an empty life and a hectic pace.
—*Fulton John Sheen*

Come to me, all you who are weary and burdened,
and I will give you rest.
—*Jesus, in Matthew 11:28, NIV*

SEPTEMBER 21

All is well with you even though everything seems to go dead wrong, if you are square with yourself. Reversely, all is not well with you although everything outwardly may seem to go right, if you are not square with yourself.
—*Mohandas K. Gandhi*

And the peace of God, which transcends all understanding, will guard your hearts and your minds in Christ Jesus.
—*Philippians 4:7, NIV*

APRIL 24

Many people among us are full of hope. . . . These peacemakers are not waiting for The Big Powers to achieve The Peace. They know that peace begins in each of us, in our hearts and homes, and that peace, like love, is often hardest to achieve with those closest to us.

—*Pat Corrick Hinton*

Above all, maintain constant love for one another, for love covers a multitude of sins.

—*1 Peter 4:8, NRSV*

SEPTEMBER 20

True peace is not merely the absence
of tension, but it is the presence of justice.
—*Martin Luther King Jr.*

Follow justice and justice alone, so that you may live
and possess the land the Lord your God is giving you.
—*Deuteronomy 16:20, NIV*

APRIL 25

If I begin to take the love of Christ
seriously, then I will work toward what is
best for my neighbor.
—*Billy Graham*

By this everyone will know that you are my disciples,
if you have love for one another.
—*John 13:35, NRSV*

SEPTEMBER 19

Bring to our troubled minds,
Uncertain and afraid,
The quiet of a steadfast faith,
Calm of a call obeyed.
—*Robert B. Y. Scott*

Those who wait for the Lord shall renew their strength,
  they shall mount up with wings like eagles,
  they shall run and not be weary,
  they shall walk and not faint.
—*Isaiah 40:31, NRSV*

APRIL 26

Pacifism is a gift. Maybe it is a gift directly passed down by our parents. Maybe it is a gift received at the end of a hard time of struggling. . . . However we receive it, God calls us to accept this gift with joy.
—*Ted Grimsrud*

No one can receive anything except what has been given from heaven.
—*John 3:27, NRSV*

SEPTEMBER 18

The probability that we may fail in the struggle ought not to deter us from the support of a cause we believe to be just.
—*Abraham Lincoln*

Wait for the Lord;
  be strong and take heart
  and wait for the Lord.
—*Psalm 27:14, NIV*

APRIL 27

The generals and fighters on both sides, in World War II, the ones who carried out the total destruction of entire cities, these were the sane ones. On the other hand, you will probably find that the pacifists and the ban-the-bomb people are, quite seriously, just as we read in *Time*, a little crazy. . . . In a society like ours, the worst insanity is to be totally without anxiety, totally "sane."
—*Thomas Merton*

God looks down from heaven on humankind
   to see if there are any who are wise,
   who seek after God.
—*Psalm 53:2, NRSV*

SEPTEMBER 17

They loved me into the kingdom of God.
They melted away the anger, the hatred,
and I accepted all the grace and all the forgiveness that the Lord
had for me, . . . and that was a great grace for me because it
healed me.
—*Michael Chandler*

I have loved you with an everlasting love;
   therefore I have continued my faithfulness to you.
—*Jeremiah 31:3b, NRSV*

APRIL 28

Why do we spend money, time, and energy to tan ourselves but hate people who are born tan? Why do we enjoy traveling around the world but resist when the world comes to us? . . . The all-loving and knowing God has brought about such differences within creation.

—*Basanti Jacobs, poster by Many Peoples Council,*
General Conference Mennonite Church

Christ gave gifts for building up the body of Christ, until all of us come to the unity of the faith and of the knowledge of the Son of God, to maturity, to the measure of the full stature of Christ.

—*Ephesians 4:11-13, NRSV, adapted*

SEPTEMBER 16

The snail gives off stillness.
The weed is blessed.
At the end of a long day, the man finds joy,
the water peace.
—*Charles Sunic*

A harvest of righteousness is sown in peace
by those who make peace.
—*James 3:18, NRSV, alternate reading*

APRIL 29

Suppose they gave a war, and no one came.
—*Charlotte Keyes, in* McCall's, *October 1966*

I have told you these things, so that in me you may have peace. In this world you will have trouble. But take heart! I have overcome the world.
—*John 16:33, NIV*

SEPTEMBER 15

To bring peace where there is trouble, love where there is hatred, abundance where there is hunger, educability where there is ignorance and illiteracy, confidence where there is doubt or uncertainty, and light where there is darkness—this is the role of true diplomacy. It is also the role of true Christian love.

—*Josiah M. Muganda, Mennonite leader, Tanzania*

Whatever you have learned or received or heard from me, or seen in me—put it into practice. And the God of peace will be with you.

—*Philippians 4:9, NIV*

APRIL 30

The conquest of war and the pursuit of social justice . . . must become our grand preoccupation and magnificent obsession.
—*Norman Cousins, in a commencement talk at Harvard Medical School, 1983*

The Lord makes wars cease to the ends of the earth;
   he breaks the bow and shatters the spear,
   he burns the shields with fire.
—*Psalm 46:9, NIV, adapted*

SEPTEMBER 14

Nonresistance is so powerful it can inspire
murderous rage from those it confronts.
—*David Hayden*

When they heard this, they were furious and gnashed their
teeth at him. But Stephen, full of the Holy Spirit, looked up
to heaven and saw the glory of God, and Jesus standing
at the right hand of God.
—*Acts 7:54-55, NIV*

MAY 1

The things that make us alike are stronger
than the things that make us different.
—*John Adams, as a father*

My purpose is that they may be encouraged in heart and united
in love, so that they may have the full riches of complete
understanding, in order that they may know the mystery
of God, namely, Christ.
—*Colossians 2:2, NIV*

SEPTEMBER 13

We know that the lion and the lamb lie
within the breasts of all. . . . May we with
tenderness, sympathy, overcoming evil
with good, be able to win the "lamb"
within those whom we meet.
—*George Fox*

How beautiful upon the mountains
   are the feet of the messenger who announces peace,
who brings good news,
   who announces salvation,
   who says to Zion, "Your God reigns."
—*Isaiah 52:7, NRSV*

MAY 2

The Old Testament word for peace (shalom) includes healing, reconciliation, and well-being. Peace is more than the absence of war; it includes the restoration of right relationship.

—*"Commentary" on Confession of Faith in a Mennonite Perspective*

Now, O Israel, what does the Lord your God require of you? Only to fear the Lord your God, to walk in all his ways, to love him, to serve the Lord your God with all your heart and with all your soul.

—*Deuteronomy 10:12, NRSV*

SEPTEMBER 12

No army can withstand the strength
of an idea whose time has come.
—*Victor Hugo*

The Lord is the strength of his people,
   a fortress of salvation for his anointed one.
—*Psalm 28:8, NIV*

MAY 3

Don't worry much yet about feeding the poor, housing the homeless, protecting the abused. . . . They are not likely to succeed unless they are grounded, one way or another, in community. Form a community first.

—*M. Scott Peck*

All who believed were together and had all things in common; they would sell their possessions and goods and distribute the proceeds to all, as any had need.

—*Acts 2:44-45, NRSV*

SEPTEMBER 11

The regenerated do not go to war,
nor engage in strife. They are the children
of peace who have beaten their swords
into plowshares and their spears
into pruning hooks.
—*Menno Simons*

Let them make peace with me,
    yes, let them make peace with me.
—*Isaiah 27:5b, NIV*

MAY 4

Let us not forget that the supreme example of nonviolent resistance to evil is the crucifixion of our Lord Jesus Christ. . . . Far from being an act of mere helpless passivity, . . . this was a free and willing acceptation of suffering in the most positive and active manner.
—*Thomas Merton*

No one has greater love than this, to lay down one's life for one's friends.
—*John 15:13, NRSV*

SEPTEMBER 10

There is not peace because there are no peacemakers, there are not peacemakers because the making of peace is at least as costly as the making of war.
—*Daniel Berrigan*

So therefore, none of you can become my disciple if you do not give up all your possessions.
—*Jesus, in Luke 14:33, NRSV*

MAY 5

Teach peace.
—*Bumper sticker*

The teaching of the wise is a fountain of life.
—*Proverbs 13:14a, NIV*

SEPTEMBER 9

Give to us peace in our time, O Lord.
—*Henry F. Chorley*

So do not throw away your confidence;
it will be richly rewarded.
—*Hebrews 10:35, NIV*

MAY 6

God has not called me to be successful.
He has called me to be faithful.
—*Mother Teresa*

Fight the good fight of the faith.
—*1 Timothy 6:12a, NIV*

SEPTEMBER 8

We cannot obtain salvation, grace, reconciliation, nor peace of the Father otherwise than through Christ Jesus.
—*Menno Simons*

Jesus said to him, "I am the way, and the truth, and the life. No one comes to the Father except through me."
—*Jesus, in John 14:6, NRSV*

MAY 7

Peace is not a thing of weakness. It calls for heroism and action. . . . The meek must be strong.
—*Stefan Zweig, Viennese poet*

With the Lord on my side I do not fear.
What can mortals do to me?
—*Psalm 118:6, NRSV*

SEPTEMBER 7

I knew someone had to take the first step,
and I made up my mind not to move.
—*Rosa Parks, who refused to move to the back of the bus,*
  Montgomery, Alabama, 1955

The effect of righteousness will be peace,
  and the result of righteousness,
  quietness and trust forever.
—*Isaiah 32:17, NRSV*

MAY 8

Once the exclusive province of the so-called peace churches, pacifism has spread to a wider base within Christianity and has enlisted support from nonreligious pacifism as well.
—*Sigurd Lokken*

Then King Darius wrote to all peoples and nations of every language throughout the whole world: "May you have abundant prosperity!"
—*Daniel 6:25, NRSV*

SEPTEMBER 6

Establishing lasting peace is the work of
education; all politics can do is keep us
out of war.
—*Maria Montessori*

Recite these commandments to your children and talk about
them when you are at home and when you are away, when you
lie down and when you rise.
—*Deuteronomy 6:7, NRSV, adapted*

MAY 9

A child [is] crying in the dark. The child's mother comes into the room and says simply, "It's all right," and the child quiets down and goes back to sleep. That trivial ordinary happening, so common in every home, has a cosmic significance! Because that's what we all want to know and experience—peace.
—*Peter Berger*

I will lie down and sleep in peace,
    for you alone, O Lord, make me dwell in safety.
—*Psalm 4:8, NIV*

SEPTEMBER 5

The same Spirit that empowered Jesus also empowers us to love enemies, to forgive rather than to seek revenge, to practice right relationships, to rely on the community of faith to settle disputes, and to resist evil without violence.

—*Confession of Faith in a Mennonite Perspective*

But I tell you who hear me: Love your enemies, do good to those who hate you.

—*Luke 6:27, NIV*

MAY 10

I dream of giving birth to a child who will
ask: "Mother, what was war?"
—*Eve Merriam*

May you see your children's children.
Peace be upon Israel!
—*Psalm 128:6, NRSV*

SEPTEMBER 4

Peace in Christian usage means right relations. To be at peace with one's self is to have all aspects of the personality working together as a unity.
—*Culbert G. Rutenber*

In everything set them an example by doing what is good. In your teaching show integrity, seriousness, and soundness of speech.
—*Titus 2:7-8a, NIV*

MAY 11

Reliance on violence is suicidal, said Jesus.
—*Harry Emerson Fosdick, in a sermon at the
League of Nations Assembly Service, 1925*

For all who take the sword will perish by the sword.
—*Matthew 26:52, NRSV*

SEPTEMBER 3

Peace, perfect peace,
   by thronging duties pressed?
To do the will of Jesus,
   this is rest.
—*Edward H. Bickersteth*

I will satisfy the weary,
   and all who are faint I will replenish.
—*Jeremiah 31:25, NRSV*

MAY 12

We need to rediscover that the daily resources of forgiveness and mercy from God are essential ingredients for the task of struggling for human justice and peace against odds that, without such help, would seem impossible to overcome.
—*Robert McAfee Brown*

I will sing of your strength, O Lord,
　in the morning I will sing of your love;
for you are my fortress,
　my refuge in times of trouble.
—*Psalm 59:16, NIV, adapted*

SEPTEMBER 2

Until now I did not believe in God. I had experienced human beings only as beasts, and I thought that, therefore, there was no love in this world. Now I am starving and you came many, many miles across the ocean to feed me. Does that not prove that there is love, and that there is a living God in spite of all hatred and distress on earth?

—*Helga Kremnitzer, Germany, 1948*

But I tell you: Love your enemies and pray for those who persecute you.

—*Matthew 5:44, NIV*

MAY 13

The person who is reconciled to God has found in the experience of honest confession and humble repentance the way to be reconciled to his fellowmen.
—*Myron Augsburger*

If there is repentance, you must forgive.
—*Jesus, in Luke 17:3b, NRSV*

SEPTEMBER 1

Nonviolence does not seek to defeat or humiliate the opponent, but to win his friendship and understanding.
—*Martin Luther King Jr.*

So if anyone is in Christ, there is a new creation: everything old has passed away; see, everything has become new!
—*2 Corinthians 5:17, NRSV*

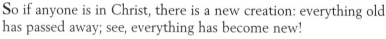

MAY 14

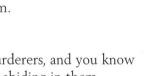

Nonviolence means avoiding not only external physical violence but also internal violence of spirit. You not only refuse to shoot a man, but you refuse to hate him.
—*Martin Luther King Jr.*

All who hate a brother or sister are murderers, and you know that murderers do not have eternal life abiding in them.
—*1 John 3:15, NRSV*

AUGUST 31

The force generated by nonviolence is infinitely greater than the force of all the arms invented by man's ingenuity.
—*Mohandas K. Gandhi*

And now faith, hope, and love abide, these three;
     and the greatest of these is love.
—*1 Corinthians 13:13, NRSV*

MAY 15

Teach us to walk the soft earth as relatives
to all that live.
—*Sioux prayer*

The seed will grow well,
 the vine will yield its fruit,
the ground will produce its crops,
 and the heavens will drop their dew.
—*Zechariah 8:12a, NIV*

AUGUST 30

Love and justice belong together like two
sides of the same coin.
—*Culbert G. Rutenber*

Defend the cause of the weak and fatherless;
   maintain the rights of the poor and oppressed.
—*Psalm 82:3, NIV*

MAY 16

An inglorious peace is better than a dishonorable war.
—*John Adams*

Since everything will be destroyed in this way, what kind of people ought you to be? You ought to live holy and godly lives.
—*2 Peter 3:11, NIV*

AUGUST 29

I know that I want to have a door in the depths of my being, a door that is not locked against the faces of all other human beings. I know that I want to be able to say, from those depths, "Naturally, come in, and come in."
—*Philip Hallie*, Lest Innocent Blood Be Shed

God is love.
—*1 John 4:8b, NIV*

MAY 17

The pioneers of a warless world are the
young men who refuse military service.
—*Albert Einstein*

Bow and sword and battle
   I will abolish from the land,
   so that all may lie down in safety.
—*Hosea 2:18b, NIV*

AUGUST 28

The application of the principle of nonresistance, from our standpoint, is easier for nations than it is for individuals. It is more difficult to apply in our relationships with one another, in the same house, church, workplace.

—Richard Bentzinger, United Methodist minister,
speech to Civilian Public Service reunion

You must understand this, my beloved: let everyone be quick to listen, slow to speak, slow to anger.

—James 1:19, NRSV

MAY 18

All we are saying, is give peace a chance.
—*Pete Seeger, Washington War Moratorium,*
  November 1969

My people will abide in a peaceful habitation,
in secure dwellings, and in quiet resting places.
—*Isaiah 32:18, NRSV*

AUGUST 27

There would be much less war if statesmen were as frank while getting us into war as they are when the war is over.

—*Woodrow Wilson, from a speech asking for declaration of war, April 2, 1917, and a speech September 5, 1919*

As Jesus approached Jerusalem and saw the city, he wept over it and said, "If you, even you, had only known on this day what would bring you peace—but now it is hidden from your eyes."

—*Luke 19:41-42, NIV, adapted*

MAY 19

When civilization is made up of millions of men and women who are at war with themselves, it is not long until communities, classes, states, and nations will be at war with one another.

—*Fulton John Sheen*

Do good to your servant
according to your word, O Lord.
—*Psalm 119:65, NIV*

AUGUST 26

Save us from weak resignation
  to the evils we deplore.
—*Harry Emerson Fosdick*

Find rest, O my soul, in God alone;
  my hope comes from him.
He alone is my rock and my salvation;
  he is my fortress, I will not be shaken.
—*Psalm 62:5-6, NIV*

MAY 20

He drew a circle that shut me out—
Heretic, rebel, a thing to flout.
But love and I had the wit to win:
We drew a circle that took him in.
—*Edwin Markham*

Go and learn what this means, "I desire mercy, not sacrifice."
For I have come to call not the righteous but sinners.
—*Jesus, in Matthew 9:13, NRSV*

AUGUST 25

God's love for his own enemies simply can't be fathomed. He draws all people to himself. We must make a choice to work toward God's goals and purposes or to put our own goals and purposes first.

—*Duane Beachy*

Strive first for the kingdom of God and his righteousness, and all these things will be given to you as well.

—*Matthew 6:33, NRSV*

MAY 21

When nothing seems to help, I go and look at a stonecutter hammering away at his rock perhaps a hundred times without as much as a crack showing in it. Yet at the hundred and first blow it will split in two, and I know it was not that blow that did it—but all that had gone before.

—*Jacob A. Riis*

The seed on good soil stands for those with a noble and good heart, who hear the word, retain it, and by persevering produce a crop.

—*Luke 8:15, NIV*

AUGUST 24

It is for us to decide whether we are going to give in to hatred, terror, and blind love of power, . . . and thus plunge our world into the abyss, or whether, restraining our savagery, we can patiently and humanely work together for interests which transcend the limits of any national or ideological community.

—*Thomas Merton*

Trust in him at all times, O people;
    pour out your hearts to him,
    for God is our refuge. *Selah*
—*Psalm 62:8, NIV*

MAY 22

Growing up, I had been taught that it was wrong to kill. Period. A Christian could have no part in violence.
—*Melodie M. Davis*

I gave them this command: Obey me, and I will be your God and you will be my people. Walk in all the ways I command you, that it may go well with you.
—*Jeremiah 7:23, NIV*

AUGUST 23

An eye for an eye and a tooth for a tooth—
that way everyone in the world will soon
be blind and toothless.
—*Teyve, in* Fiddler on the Roof

When the ways of people please the Lord,
  he causes even their enemies to be at peace with them.
—*Proverbs 16:7, NRSV*

MAY 23

Pray for your enemy. One concrete way is to pray the Lord's Prayer for them.
—*Anonymous*

If you forgive others their trespasses, your heavenly Father will also forgive you; but if you do not forgive others, neither will your Father forgive your trespasses.
—*Matthew 6:14-15, NRSV*

AUGUST 22

After looking at the lives of many peace-makers and trying to understand what keeps them going, it seems to me that the only thing that will sustain us to be peacemakers throughout our lives is prayer. . . . The more central prayer becomes to our life as peacemakers, the longer we will be able to act as children of God.
—*Chuck Walters*

Be still, and know that I am God;
   I will be exalted among the nations,
   I will be exalted in the earth.
—*Psalm 46:10, NIV*

MAY 24

Many Christians say we must fight to defend our freedom to worship God, but Jesus never promised us that or any other political freedom. Jesus Christ is our freedom!

—*Duane Beachy*

If the Son sets you free, you will be free indeed.
—*John 8:36, NIV*

AUGUST 21

Holiness is health" is true when the civil war within has ended by an experience of holiness.

—*Myron Augsburger*

Nevertheless, I will bring health and healing to it; I will heal my people and will let them enjoy abundant peace and security.

—*Jeremiah 33:6, NIV*

MAY 25

Blessed are they who translate every good thing they know into action, for ever-higher truths shall be revealed unto them.
—*Peace Pilgrim*

Then you will call, and the Lord will answer;
   you will cry for help, and he will say: Here am I.
"If you do away with the yoke of oppression,
   with the pointing finger and malicious talk,
and if you spend yourselves in behalf of the hungry
   and satisfy the needs of the oppressed,
then your light will rise in the darkness,
   and your night will become like the noonday."
—*Isaiah 58:9-10, NIV*

AUGUST 20

As man eliminates sin, he eliminates
suffering; as he loves God, he ceases to
hate his fellowman and therefore engages
in fewer wars.
—*Fulton John Sheen*

Put away from you all bitterness and wrath and anger and
wrangling and slander, together with all malice, and be kind
to one another.
—*Ephesians 4:31-32, NRSV*

MAY 26

If we believe in the final victory of God over evil forces, then we should be willing to wait for it. We do not have to try to hurry up God's victory by causing suffering to our present enemies, or by killing them.
—*Lois Barrett*

Praise be to the Lord, to God our Savior, who daily bears our burdens. *Selah*
—*Psalm 68:19, NIV*

AUGUST 19

The only way to enact changes of opinion for peace and progress is through education and long-range peaceful settlements. These may take longer, but they do not take lives.

—*Jeannette Rankin, the lone U.S. Congress member who voted against entering World War II*

Blessed are they who keep the Lord's statutes
and seek him with all their heart.
—*Psalm 119:2, NIV, adapted*

MAY 27

Who gives himself with his alms,
 feeds three—
Himself, his hungering neighbor, and me.
—*James Russell Lowell, based on Jesus' words*

When you give a banquet, invite the poor, the crippled,
the lame, and the blind. And you will be blessed, because they
cannot repay you, for you will be repaid at the resurrection
of the righteous.
—*Luke 14:13-14, NRSV*

AUGUST 18

Iron and metal spears and swords we leave
to those who, alas, regard human blood and
swine's blood about alike. He that is wise,
let him judge what I mean.
—*Menno Simons*

So God created humankind in his image, in the image of God
he created them; male and female he created them.
—*Genesis 1:27, NRSV*

MAY 28

To be loved, we must be lovable; to be lovable, we must be good; to be good, we must know goodness; and to know goodness, is to love God, and neighbor, and everybody in the world.
—*Fulton John Sheen*

Each of us must please our neighbor for the good purpose of building up the neighbor.
—*Romans 15:2, NRSV*

AUGUST 17

There never has been, nor ever will be, any
such thing as a good war or a bad peace.
—*Benjamin Franklin*

Your country is desolate,
your cities burned with fire;
your fields are being stripped
by foreigners right before you.
—*Isaiah 1:7a, NIV*

MAY 29

The supreme happiness of life is the
conviction that we are loved.
—*Victor Hugo*

For God so loved the world that he gave his one and only Son,
that whoever believes in him shall not perish but have eternal
life.
—*John 3:16, NIV*

AUGUST 16

It isn't enough just to do right things and say right things—you must also think right things before your life can come into harmony.
—*Peace Pilgrim*

The Lord knows our thoughts.
—*Psalm 94:11a, NRSV*

MAY 30

Show us your light, O God,
That we may fight
For peace with peace
And not with war.

—*On gravestone of Nicholas Peters, a poet and Canadian Air Force
  officer killed in battle in Germany*

The path of the righteous is like the light of dawn,
  which shines brighter and brighter until full day.
—*Proverbs 4:18, NRSV*

AUGUST 15

All who affirm the use of violence admit it is only a means to achieve justice and peace. But peace and justice are nonviolence, . . . the final end of history. Those who abandon nonviolence have no sense of history. Rather, they are bypassing history, freezing history, betraying history.
—*Andre Trocmé*

Let us not grow weary in doing what is right, for we will reap at harvest-time, if we do not give up.
—*Galatians 6:9, NRSV*

MAY 31

Nonviolence succeeds only when we have
a real living faith in God.
—*Mohandas K. Gandhi*

Those of steadfast mind you keep in peace—
   in peace because they trust in you.
—*Isaiah 26:3, NRSV*

AUGUST 14

The first peace, which is the most important, is that which comes within the souls of the people when they realize their relationship, their oneness with the universe and all its powers, and when they realize that at the center of the universe dwells the Great Spirit, and that this center is really everywhere; it is within each of us.

—*Black Elk, about the Oglala Sioux*
(© Univ. of Okla.; see Credits)

All the earth bows down to you;
    they sing praise to you,
    they sing praise to your name. *Selah*
—*Psalm 66:4, NIV*

JUNE 1

To allow oneself to be carried away by
a multitude of conflicting concerns, to
surrender to too many demands, to commit oneself to too many
projects, . . . is to succumb to violence. . . . The frenzy of the
activist neutralizes his work for peace. It destroys his own inner
capacity for peace.
—*Thomas Merton*

So then, a sabbath rest still remains for the people of God.
—*Hebrews 4:9, NRSV*

AUGUST 13

Love, as revealed and interpreted in the life and death of Jesus Christ, involves more than we have yet seen, and is the only power by which evil can be overthrown and the only sufficient basis for human society.
—*International Fellowship of Reconciliation*

Hope does not disappoint us, because God has poured out his love into our hearts by the Holy Spirit, whom he has given us.
—*Romans 5:5, NIV*

JUNE 2

When . . . people are interested in the raising of a family, the cultivation of virtues and the salvation of their souls, they act as a balance wheel against the power-motive of politics. But when both the state and the people give supremacy to politics, the stabilizing influence of society is lost, and with it come civil strife and discord and war.

—*Fulton John Sheen*

Jesus gave himself for our sins to set us free from the present evil age, according to the will of our God and Father.

—*Galatians 1:4, NRSV, adapted*

AUGUST 12

One cannot prepare for war unless he has an enemy.

—*Jeannette Rankin, the lone U.S. Congress member who voted against entering World War II*

Deliver me, O Lord, from evildoers;
  protect me from those who are violent.
—*Psalm 140:1, NRSV*

JUNE 3

When forgiveness denies that there is anger, acts as if it never happened, smiles as though it never hurts, fakes as though it is all forgotten— . . . it is not forgiveness. It's a magical fantasy.
—*David Augsburger*

If those who are nothing think they are something, they deceive themselves.
—*Galatians 6:3, NRSV*

AUGUST 11

Create in us the splendor
  that dawns when hearts are kind,
That knows not race nor color
  as boundaries of the mind.
—*S. Ralph Harlow*

For in the one Spirit we were all baptized into one body—
Jews or Greeks, slave or free—and we were all made to drink
of one Spirit.
—*1 Corinthians 12:13, NRSV*

JUNE 4

Nonresistance means "not resisting." Our example is Jesus, who endured accusation and abuse without retaliating. Jesus did sometimes confront wrongdoers, but he did so in a nonviolent way that shows us how to overcome evil with good.

—*"Commentary" on Confession of Faith in a Mennonite Perspective*

He was despised and rejected by others;
   a man of suffering and acquainted with infirmity.
—*Isaiah 53:3a, NRSV*

AUGUST 10

It's mighty hard to find everlasting peace as long as there are more dogs than bones.
—*In* Salt and Pepper

Live in peace with each other.
—*1 Thessalonians 5:13b, NIV*

JUNE 5

You are not likely to be able to contribute
much to peacemaking until you yourself
become a skilled peacemaker.
—*M. Scott Peck*

You hypocrite, first take the log out of your own eye, and then
you will see clearly to take the speck out of your neighbor's eye.
—*Matthew 7:5, NRSV*

AUGUST 9

I know the human race is not going to suddenly be converted to Christ, but that does not keep me from preaching [Christ]. I also know the nations are not going to suddenly lay down their arms, but that does not keep us from doing all we can before it is too late.
—*Billy Graham*

The wolf and the lamb will feed together,
   and the lion will eat straw like the ox,
   but dust will be the serpent's food.
They will neither harm nor destroy
   on all my holy mountain," says the Lord.
—*Isaiah 65:25, NIV*

JUNE 6

Isn't it wonderful to have a method of struggle that makes it possible to stand up against an unjust system, fight it with all of your might, never accept it, and yet not stoop to violence and hatred in the process?
—*Martin Luther King Jr.*

Why should I fear when evil days come,
  when wicked deceivers surround me.
—*Psalm 49:5, NIV*

AUGUST 8

In the Second World War when the Jews were all being gassed, lots of us didn't do or say anything, because we said we couldn't do anything about it. But those who did speak and act, without success, are still celebrated as people who gave history hope.

—*Henri Nouwen*

For the righteous will never be moved;
　they will be remembered forever.
—*Psalm 112:6, NRSV*

JUNE 7

Peace is the feeling knowing the sun will
come out even while it's raining.
—*Judith, age 11*

As long as the earth endures, seedtime and harvest, cold and
heat, summer and winter, day and night will never cease.
—*Genesis 8:22, NIV*

AUGUST 7

God calls you to destroy your machines
of war, to leave your violent occupations,
and find your security in him alone.
—*Duane Beachy*

Now to God who by the power at work within us is able
to accomplish abundantly far more than all we can ask or
imagine, to him be glory in the church and in Christ Jesus
to all generations, forever and ever. Amen.
—*Ephesians 3:20-21, NRSV, adapted*

JUNE 8

If we are to reach real peace in this world,
. . . we shall have to begin with children;
and if they will grow up in their natural innocence, . . . we shall
go from love to love and peace to peace, until at last all the
corners of the world are covered with that peace and love
for which consciously or unconsciously the whole world is
hungering.
—*Mohandas K. Gandhi*

On earth peace among those whom God favors.
—*Luke 2:14b, NRSV, adapted*

AUGUST 6

If you alone of all the nation shall decide one way, and that way be the right way according to your convictions of the right, you have done your duty by yourself and by your country—hold up your head! You have nothing to be ashamed of.
—*Mark Twain*

Blessed are the peacemakers,
   for they will be called children of God.
—*Matthew 5:9, NRSV*

JUNE 9

Is not fear one of the major causes of war?
We say that war is a consequence of hate,
but close scrutiny reveals this sequence: first fear, then hate,
then war, and finally deeper hatred.
—*Martin Luther King Jr.*

What causes fights and quarrels among you? Don't they come
from your desires that battle within you?
—*James 4:1, NIV*

AUGUST 5

To serve is the answer to the always-so-disturbing questions of the meaning and the fulfillment of our life on earth.

—*Erling Eidem, Archbishop Emeritus of the State Lutheran Church in Sweden, upon the death of Dag Hammarskjöld*

Truly I tell you, just as you did it to one of the least of these who are members of my family, you did it to me.

—*Matthew 25:40, NRSV*

JUNE 10

The spiral of responding to violence with violence is like a whirlpool in a river, [Vernard Eller] says. As the water pours in, it whirls faster and faster. The only way to stop the whirlpool is to place a solid rock in the middle. Peacemakers are called to be rocks in the whirlpool of violence.

—*Susan Classen*

Who is the Rock except our God?
It is God who arms me with strength
   and makes my way perfect.
—*Psalm 18:31b-32, NIV*

AUGUST 4

Jesus help us live in peace;
from our blindness set us free.
Fill us with your healing love.
Help us live in unity.
—*Gerald Derstine*

This is love: that we walk in obedience to God's commands.
As you have heard from the beginning, his command is that you
walk in love.
—*2 John 6, NIV, adapted*

JUNE 11

A good end cannot sanctify evil means; nor must we ever do evil, that good may come of it. We are too ready to retaliate, rather than forgive or gain by love and information. . . . Force may subdue, but love gains.
—*William Penn*

Turn from evil and do good;
   then you will dwell in the land forever.
—*Psalm 37:27, NIV*

AUGUST 3

The test of our progress is not whether we add more to the abundance of those who have much; it is whether we provide enough for those who have too little.

—*Franklin D. Roosevelt, Second Inaugural Address, January 1937*

You shall not strip your vineyard bare, or gather the fallen grapes of your vineyard; you shall leave them for the poor and the alien: I am the Lord your God.

—*Leviticus 19:10, NRSV*

More than an end to war, we want an end
to the beginnings of all wars—yes, an end
to this brutal, inhuman, and thoroughly impractical method
of settling the differences between governments.
—*Franklin Delano Roosevelt*

There God broke the flashing arrows,
   the shields and the swords,
   the weapons of war. *Selah*
—*Psalm 76:3, NIV, adapted*

AUGUST 2

Nonresistance is to aim for the most,
the best, the highest.
—*Richard Bentzinger, United Methodist minister,
speech to Civilian Public Service reunion, adapted*

Bear with each other and forgive whatever grievances you may
have against one another. Forgive as the Lord forgave you. And
over all these virtues put on love, which binds them all together
in perfect unity.
—*Colossians 3:13-14, NIV*

JUNE 13

I believe that the Christian especially has a responsibility to work for peace in our world. Christians may well find themselves working and agreeing with nonbelievers on an issue like peace.
—*Billy Graham*

Pray for the peace of Jerusalem:
  "May those who love you be secure.
May there be peace within your walls
  and security within your citadels."
—*Psalm 122:6-7, NIV*

AUGUST 1

It is God and God alone who is justified in using the credo "Peace Through Strength."
—*Peter Monkres*

The Lord will destroy on this mountain
    the shroud that is cast over all peoples,
    the sheet that is spread over all nations;
    he will swallow up death forever.
Then the Lord God will wipe away the tears from all faces;
    and the disgrace of his people he will take away
        from all the earth.
—*Isaiah 25:7-8, NRSV, adapted*

JUNE 14

When you become identified with the
poor, the gluttons, the drunkards, . . . you
experience the same opposition Jesus did.
—*David Hayden*

If you close your ear to the cry of the poor,
    you will cry out and not be heard.
—*Proverbs 21:13, NRSV*

JULY 31

For nobler men may yet redeem our clay
When we and war together, one wise day,
Have passed away.
—*Vera Brittain*

The Lord is exalted over all the nations,
   his glory above the heavens.
—*Psalm 113:4, NIV*

JUNE 15

Do not expect your peace to come from
the mouths of [others].
—*Amy Carmichael*

There is deceit in the hearts of those who plot evil,
   but joy for those who promote peace.
—*Proverbs 12:20, NIV*

JULY 30

Love is more powerful than any bullet.
—*Vernon Miller, Conscientious Objector,
World War II*

Hatred stirs up dissension,
   but love covers over all wrongs.
—*Proverbs 10:12, NIV*

JUNE 16

The Prince of Peace is Christ Jesus; his kingdom is the kingdom of peace, his word is the word of peace, his body is the body of peace; his children are the seed of peace. In short, with this King, and in his kingdom and reign, it is nothing but peace.
—*Menno Simons, 1552*

The whole law is summed up in a single commandment, "You shall love your neighbor as yourself."
—*Galatians 5:14, NRSV*

JULY 29

No one has a right to sit down and feel
hopeless. There's too much work to do.
—*Dorothy Day*

Commit your way to the Lord;
 trust in him and he will do this:
He will make your righteousness shine like the dawn,
 the justice of your cause like the noonday sun.
—*Psalm 37:5-6, NIV*

Love does not allow one to withdraw from
evil but goes into the very heart of an evil
situation and attempts to rectify it.
—*Gordon D. Kaufman*

God ransoms me unharmed
   from the battle waged against me,
   even though many oppose me.
—*Psalm 55:18, NIV, adapted*

JULY 28

We do not see God in contemplation—we know him by love.
—*Thomas Merton*

Whoever obeys God's word, truly in this person the love of God has reached perfection.
—*1 John 2:5a, NRSV, adapted*

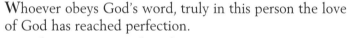

JUNE 18

Let the peace-loving people . . . light their
candle and put it on a hill, so that it can
shine beyond their borders.
—*Josiah M. Muganda, Mennonite leader, Tanzania*

The Lord grants peace to your borders
and satisfies you with the finest of wheat.
—*Psalm 147:14, NIV, adapted*

JULY 27

The nonviolent peacemaker's quest is to discover creative approaches to conflict situations that are compatible with the self-imposed limits of nonviolent peacemaking.
—*Ronald C. Arnett*

As a prisoner for the Lord, then, I urge you to live a life worthy of the calling you have received. Be completely humble and gentle; be patient, bearing with one another in love.
—*Ephesians 4:1-2, NIV*

My conscience is captive to the Word
of God. I cannot and will not recant
anything. . . . God help me. Amen.
—*Martin Luther, in his defense at the Diet of Worms*

The eyes of the Lord are on the righteous
  and his ears are attentive to their prayer,
  but the face of the Lord is against those who do evil.
—*1 Peter 3:12, NIV*

JULY 26

Communication is the most important element of family life because it is basic to loving relationships. It is the energy that fuels the caring, giving, sharing, and affirming. Without genuine sharing of ourselves, we cannot know one another's needs and fears. Good communication is what makes all the rest of it work.

—*Dolores Curran*

How very good and pleasant it is
when kindred live together in unity!
—*Psalm 133:1, NRSV*

JUNE 20

He is a man of real worth who feels no regret when others take no note of him.
—*Confucius*

Mercy, peace and love be yours in abundance.
—*Jude 1:2, NIV*

JULY 25

Peace awareness doesn't develop all at once. We start to think seriously about peace the moment we take time to listen: . . . to history, to those of a different generation; . . . to our own deeper selves, to God; . . . to those who cry out because they are poor and hungry.
—*Pat Corrick Hinton*

Hear the word of the Lord,
    you rulers of Sodom;
listen to the law of our God,
    you people of Gomorrah!
—*Isaiah 1:10, NIV*

JUNE 21

Every world war is a turbulent ocean made up of the confluent streams of millions of little wars inside the minds and hearts of unhappy people.

—*Fulton John Sheen*

The Lord himself goes before you and will be with you; he will never leave you nor forsake you. Do not be afraid; do not be discouraged.

—*Deuteronomy 31:8, NIV*

JULY 24

As Christians our job is not to support either side, but to be a different type of community—a community in which love, reconciliation, and disarmament become the mode of living.
—*Michael Garde, native of Ireland, peaceworker*

Whoever is not against us is for us. For truly I tell you, whoever gives you a cup of water to drink because you bear the name of Christ will by no means lose the reward.
—*Mark 9:40-41, NRSV*

JUNE 22

True pacifism is not unrealistic submission
to an evil power. . . . It is rather a
courageous confrontation with evil
by the power of love.
—*Martin Luther King Jr.*

Do not envy the violent
   and do not choose any of their ways;
for the perverse are an abomination to the Lord,
   but the upright are in his confidence.
—*Proverbs 3:31-32, NRSV*

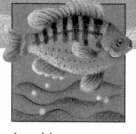

JULY 23

Humility is a trait that frees us from calling attention to ourselves. . . . We are freed, in humbly accepting God's love and care for us, to offer that same kind of benevolence and hospitality to our neighbors.
—*James G. Kirk*

Humble yourselves before the Lord, and he will lift you up.
—*James 4:10, NIV*

We praise thee, Lord, for gentle souls
  who live
In love and peace, who bear with no complaint
All wounds and wrongs; who pity and forgive;
Each one of these, Most High, shall be thy saint.
—*St. Francis of Assisi*

The Lord's servant was oppressed, and he was afflicted,
  yet he did not open his mouth;
like a lamb that is led to the slaughter,
  and like a sheep that before its shearers is silent,
  so he did not open his mouth.
—*Isaiah 53:7, NRSV, adapted*

JULY 22

There never was a war that was not inward;
I must fight till I have conquered in myself
what causes war.
—*Marianne Moore*

Draw near to God, and he will draw near to you. Cleanse your
hands, you sinners, and purify your hearts, you double-minded.
—*James 4:8, NRSV*

Do not think that you can show your love
for Christ by hating those who seem to be
his enemies on earth.
—*Thomas Merton*

We love because God first loved us.
—*1 John 4:19, NIV, adapted*

JULY 21

I pledge allegiance to the World, to cherish every living thing, to care for earth and sea and air, with peace and freedom everywhere.
—*Lillian Genser, Women's International League for Peace and Freedom*

Are not two sparrows sold for a penny? Yet not one of them will fall to the ground apart from the will of your Father. . . . So don't be afraid; you are worth more than many sparrows.
—*Matthew 10:29, 31, NIV*

JUNE 25

I have seen that we must seek the good of the whole human race, and not just the good of any one nation or race.
—*Billy Graham*

For all who are led by the Spirit of God are children of God.
—*Romans 8:14, NRSV*

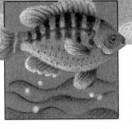

JULY 20

So when I first met some pacifist Christians, it was a big shock for me. They turned my world upside down. They said they had not fought but had obeyed God. They had been critical of their own government and had been praying for the Japanese people during the war. It was a revelation for me. Scales fell from my eyes, and I could finally see the work of Christ.

—*Yorifumi Yaguchi*

The fruit of the Spirit is love, joy, peace, patience, kindness, generosity, faithfulness, gentleness, and self-control.

—*Galatians 5:22-23, NRSV*

JUNE 26

The peacemaker's own peace is important. Unless we know the love of God as a reconciling experience in our own lives, how can we believe that reconciliation is possible in the life of the world?

—*Edward Leroy Long Jr.*

May the God of hope fill you with all joy and peace as you trust in him, so that you may overflow with hope by the power of the Holy Spirit.

—*Romans 15:13, NIV*

JULY 19

The only message I have to the world is:
We are not allowed to kill innocent people.
Our plight is very primitive from a Christian point of view. . . .
Thou shalt not kill. . . . Everything today comes down to that.
—*Daniel Berrigan*

You have heard that it was said to those of ancient times, "You shall not murder"; and "whoever murders shall be liable to judgment." But I say to you that if you are angry with a brother or sister, you will be liable to judgment.
—*Matthew 5:21a-22a, NRSV*

JUNE 27

If wars begin in the minds of persons, can
wars be stopped there, with the right logic?
—*John Oliver Nelson*

How great a forest is set ablaze by a small fire! And the tongue
is a fire. The tongue is placed among our members as a world
of iniquity.
—*James 3:5b-6a, NRSV*

JULY 18

Live the present. Do the things you know need to be done. Do all the good you can each day. The future will unfold.
—*Peace Pilgrim*

Therefore do not worry about tomorrow, for tomorrow will worry about itself.
—*Matthew 6:34a, NIV*

JUNE 28

If mankind does not end war, war will end mankind.

—*Harry Emerson Fosdick*

I stretch out my hands to you, O Lord;
my soul thirsts for you like a parched land. *Selah*
—*Psalm 143:6, NRSV, adapted*

JULY 17

People are called to peacemaking in different ways. [For example,] it is rare that God will call a mother of two young children to go to jail as a peace activist.
—*M. Scott Peck*

We have received not the spirit of the world, but the Spirit that is from God, so that we may understand the gifts bestowed on us by God.
—*1 Corinthians 2:12, NRSV*

JUNE 29

Nonresistance is a call to excellence, based on the Scripture "Thou shalt love the Lord thy God with all thy heart, . . . soul and mind and strength." Jesus was giving us a call to excellence.

—*Richard Bentzinger, United Methodist minister, speech to Civilian Public Service reunion*

Be perfect, therefore, as your heavenly Father is perfect.
—*Matthew 5:48, NRSV*

JULY 16

I do not believe the greatest threat to our future is from bombs or guided missiles. I don't think our civilization will die that way. I think it will die when we no longer care—when the spiritual forces that make us wish to be right and noble die in the hearts of men.

—Lawrence Gould

Only be careful, and watch yourselves closely so that you do not forget the things your eyes have seen or let them slip from your heart as long as you live. Teach them to your children and to their children after them.

—Deuteronomy 4:9, NIV

JUNE 30

Only love . . . can cast out the fear which
is the root of all war.
—*Thomas Merton*

See what love the Father has given us, that we should be called
children of God; and that is what we are. The reason the world
does not know us is that it did not know him.
—*1 John 3:1, NRSV*

JULY 15

Love is the subtlest force in the world.
—*Mohandas K. Gandhi*

Therefore be imitators of God, as beloved children, and live
in love, as Christ loved us and gave himself up for us, a fragrant
offering and sacrifice to God.
—*Ephesians 5:1-2, NRSV*

JULY 1

To be a patriot, one had to say, and keep on saying, "Our country, right or wrong. . . ." Have you not perceived that that phrase is an insult to the nation?
—*Mark Twain*

For in Christ Jesus you are all children of God through faith.
—*Galatians 3:26, NRSV*

JULY 14

The way to peace will be the way of the cross for those who choose to be peacemakers. It was for Jesus, and it will be for all those who follow his path.
—*Jim Wallis*

Then Jesus told his disciples, "If any want to become my followers, let them deny themselves and take up their cross and follow me."
—*Matthew 16:24, NRSV*

JULY 2

We cannot save our skins without saving our souls. We cannot heal the mess we have made of the world without undergoing some kind of spiritual healing.
—*M. Scott Peck*

Listen carefully to the voice of the Lord your God, . . . for I am the Lord who heals you.
—*Exodus 15:26, NIV*

JULY 13

A peacemaker holds tenaciously to the belief that it is possible to reduce or to overcome the contrast between our yearning for peace and the reliance we place on war as a means of protecting human achievements.

—*Edward Leroy Long Jr.*

If your enemies are hungry, feed them; if they are thirsty, give them something to drink; for by doing this you will heap burning coals on their heads.

—*Romans 12:20, NRSV*

JULY 3

The motive, if you are to find inner peace, must be an outgoing motive. The secret of life is being of service.
—*Peace Pilgrim*

Every good and perfect gift is from above, coming down from the Father of the heavenly lights, who does not change like shifting shadows.
—*James 1:17, NIV*

JULY 12

O Divine Master, grant that I may not so
    much seek
  to be consoled as to console,
  to be understood as to understand,
  to be loved as to love;
for it is in giving that we receive,
it is in pardoning that we are pardoned,
and it is in dying that we are born to eternal life.
—*St. Francis of Assisi*

For those who want to save their life will lose it, and those who
lose their life for my sake, and for the sake of the gospel, will
save it.
—*Mark 8:35, NRSV*

JULY 4

I hope that you will allow me to say . . .
that God is not interested merely in the
freedom of black men and brown men and yellow men; God is
interested in the freedom of the whole human race.
—*Martin Luther King Jr.*

So if the Son makes you free, you will be free indeed.
—*John 8:36, NRSV*

JULY 11

Lord, make me an instrument of Your peace;
   where there is hatred, let me sow love;
   where there is injury, pardon;
   where there is discord, union;
   where there is doubt, faith;
   where there is despair, hope;
   where there is darkness, light;
   and where there is sadness, joy.
—*St. Francis of Assisi*

The Lord said to Ananias, "Go!. . . I will show him how much
he must suffer for my name."
—*Acts 9:15a-16, NIV*

JULY 5

We children of the world declare peace on
the future! . . . Grown-ups of the world,
join us; grab hold of our smiles and imagine. . . . Together peace
is possible!

—*Seventh-grade class of Palms Junior High,*
  West Los Angeles, California

Truly I tell you, whoever does not receive the kingdom of God
as a little child will never enter it.

—*Luke 18:17, NRSV*

JULY 10

He prayeth well, who loveth well
Both man and bird and beast.
He prayeth best, who loveth best
All things, both great and small;
For the dear God who loveth us,
He made and loveth all.
—*Samuel Taylor Coleridge*

The commandment we have from God is this: those who love
God must love their brothers and sisters also.
—*1 John 4:21, NRSV, adapted*

JULY 6

Instead of thinking of peace as a *state* in which hostile conflict is absent or in which tranquil concord is present, the third way of understanding peace views it as an *activity*: the activity of cultivating agreements.
—*Gray Cox*

Again, I tell you that if two of you on earth agree about anything you ask for, it will be done for you by my Father in heaven.
—*Jesus, in Matthew 18:19, NIV*

JULY 9

The love of our neighbor in all its fullness
simply means being able to say, . . . What
are you going through?
—*Simone Weil*

Even though I walk
   through the valley of the shadow of death,
I will fear no evil,
   for you are with me.
—*Psalm 23:4a, NIV, addressing the Lord*

JULY 7

It is not our politics and our economics which have to be changed first. . . . It is the wars within that have to be stopped.
—*Fulton John Sheen*

The wisdom from above is first pure, then peaceable, gentle, willing to yield, full of mercy and good fruits, without a trace of partiality or hypocrisy.
—*James 3:17, NRSV*

JULY 8

No man is an island, entire of itself; every man is a piece of the continent, a part of the main.
—*John Donne*

I have given them the glory that you gave me, that they may be one as we are one: I in them and you in me.
—*John 17:22-23, NIV*